Southwark Fair

Samuel Adamson was Pearson Writer in Residence at the Bush Theatre, London, in 1997/8 and has taught in the Department of Theatre Studies at Duke University, North Carolina. His plays include *Clocks and Whistles* (Bush Theatre), *Grace Note* (Peter Hall Company/Old Vic), *The Playhousekeepers* (Private Drama), *Drink, Dance, Laugh and Lie* (Bush Theatre/Channel 4), and, for radio, *Tomorrow Week* (Catherine Bailey Ltd/BBC Radio 3). In 2005 he contributed to the *24 Hour Plays* at the Old Vic. His adaptations include Ibsen's *Pillars of the Community* (National Theatre, Lyttelton) and *A Doll's House* (Southwark Playhouse tenth anniversary production), Chekhov's *Three Sisters* (Oxford Stage Company UK tour/Whitehall Theatre) and *The Cherry Orchard* (OSC UK tour/Riverside Studios), Schnitzler's *Professor Bernhardi* (Dumbfounded Theatre/Arcola Theatre/Radio 3), and Bernhard Studlar's *Vienna Dreaming* (National Theatre Studio).

SAMUEL ADAMSON

Southwark Fair

faber and faber

First published in 2006
by Faber and Faber Limited
3 Queen Square London WC1N 3AU

Typeset by Country Setting, Kingsdown, Kent CT14 8ES
Printed in England by Mackays of Chatham plc, Chatham, Kent

A CIP record for this book
is available from the British Library

ISBN 0–571–23021–0
978–0–571 23021–1

2 4 6 8 10 9 7 5 3 1

For Richard

and Craig
high above the briers

Thanks to Nicholas Hytner, Lucy Davies,
Toby Frow, Talya Klein (for the mix tape),
Katie Haines and Nick Drake

Southwark Fair was first presented in the Cottesloe auditorium of the National Theatre, London, on 10 February 2006. The cast was as follows:

Simon Rory Kinnear
May Margaret Tyzack
Aurek Michael Legge
Alexander Rhashan Stone
Angus Simon Gleeson
Patrick Con O'Neill
Toni Madeleine Potter

Directed by Nicholas Hytner
Designed by Giles Cadle
Lighting design by Paule Constable
Sound design by Rich Walsh
Music by Grant Olding

Characters

Simon

May

Aurek

Alexander

Angus

Patrick

Toni

Note

If 'Ken Livingstone' is obscure,
replace throughout with 'the Mayor'

SOUTHWARK FAIR

Act One

ONE

Morning. Outdoor tables at a coffee shop on Tooley Street, near London Bridge Station.

Simon and May are at separate tables. Simon is thirty-two. He is wearing a Cockfighter of Bermondsey T-shirt. He has a tattoo on his arm: blue-black, tribal. May is very old. She is drinking coffee. She has a thick book open on her table. A cloth shoulder-bag is on the ground next to her.

May Psst. The new trainee *barista* is from Poland.

May is South African; the accent is only just discernible.

Simon How do you know?

Simon is English.

May Complain for me.

Simon No.

May That's right, I forgot. You're frightened of trainee *baristas*.

Simon You've got your own pins, May: use 'em.

May You could talk to him about Auschwitz.

Simon Because he's Polish?

May Yes, because he's Polish. The coffee's bitter.

Simon It's no different.

May Tell him.

Simon It tastes exactly the same as last time. You can't get them to change it, it'd be like complaining about the longevity of Cher or the theme tune to *The Archers*.

May Why aren't you in a suit?

Simon I'm bunking off so I can meet the man I had sex with when I was fourteen during the interval of a summer school production of *A Midsummer Night's Dream*. We're having lunch at the Chop House.

A Waiter comes out with a cappuccino. He is twenty-four. On his T-shirt are the words 'Trainee Barista' in big letters. He serves the coffee to Simon.

May (*to the Waiter*) And what time is this wedding?

Waiter Ten forty-five.

The Waiter's accent sounds Canadian-as-a-second-language. A phone rings, off.

May That'll be the phone, dear.

The Waiter exits. The ringing stops. Beat.

Chops?

Simon Maybe.

May With a child-molester?

Simon What? No.

May He's five or six years your senior?

Simon We're the same age.

May Not much of a difference now, but *then* . . .

Simon You're barking up the wrong tree. We were teenagers. We consented, we fumbled. What are you reading?

May This is a biography of Eleanor Marx. Do you know who she was?

Simon Karl's wife?

May Daughter.

Simon It's very thick.

May It's Volume One.

Simon What did she do?

May Pumped her blood through the working class in the 1880s. There's a project they're developing. They saw me in that episode of *Catweazle*, they think I have the right dark, Jewish features. Marx's father converted but Eleanor learned Yiddish to work in the East End. You should have heard of Marx's daughter. She was known as 'Tussy'. A film could bring her back.

Simon I see.

May So I'm reading her biography.

Simon Yes.

May They're considering me. They saw me in that episode of *Catweazle*, they thought I had her unbeautiful Prussian face.

Simon Right.

> *A Man enters. He's wearing a business suit, with a buttonhole. He is forty-five. He weaves through the tables on his way inside. He trips over May's bag. He tries to stop his fall but crashes into Simon's table. Simon stands immediately to help, but is unclear as to what to do.*

May Heavens. Are you all right?

Man Yes. Fine.

> *The Man is English.*

Simon You sure?

Man (*nodding, irritated*) Thanks.

> *He looks about – any witnesses?*

Simon It's all right. No one saw.

Man (*to May*) This is a walkway. People walk along it.

He exits inside.

May Quite a tumble.

They give in to laughter.

Simon Do you know who that was?

May shakes her head.

The Deputy Mayor. Alexander Weekes.

May It wasn't.

Simon The GLA member for Lambeth and Southwark just went arse over tit over your bag, May.

May I bought that bag in Bengal.

They drink their coffee.

I didn't even know we had a Deputy Mayor.

She closes her eyes. Perhaps she's asleep.

What's your middle name, Simon? I'd like to put you in my will.

Simon Don't be stupid.

May I'm not wealthy.

Simon I earn enough. I'd feel guilty if I wasted it.

May Discipline yourself. Create something permanent. A foundation for flautists, a refuge for abused boys.

Simon You do it.

May No, I want my money to go to you. Then it's yours and you can do whatever you like with it. That's how money works.

Simon I don't want to be in your will.

May You're going to lose your job.

Simon I never take the day off.

May Did you say food-poisoning?

Simon I'm not a fucking idiot.

May I disagree. Your new suit is too big. I saw you leaving the building on Friday, swimming in it.

Beat.

If the truth is that the person you're meeting for lunch was a man when you were a boy, killing him mightn't be so complicated. You'd just need poison mushrooms, like Caligula's sister. If he was older than you – eighteen when you were fourteen, or twenty-three – then it's justifiable. You'll find your way through the fallout. I'd say you told me when you moved next door. I'd testify for the last three years I've heard screams from your nightmares while I was up making Horlicks.

Simon I haven't got any mushrooms. I don't hate anyone. He's the same age.

May I'd testify.

Simon There are no ladybirds on my window boxes.

May Have you used pesticide?

Simon Yeah.

May You've straitjacketed them. It clamps their wings. They can't fly or feed – on the aphids you removed from the food-chain, numbskull. It's a long, diabolical death.

The Waiter comes out.

Don't think I haven't seen the champagne you're drinking in there. I'll be complaining to Marco.

He picks up her cup.

Acrid.

Simon Do you have, um, a tomato and mozzarella panini coming for me?

Waiter I don't know – do I?

Simon Yes . . . you do.

Waiter OK, then.

He exits.

May Why do you cower in front of them? Don't cower.

Beat.

What's his name, the beast from *A Midsummer Night's Dream*?

Simon Patrick. Patrick Mulligan.

May Chops, with a paedophile named Patrick, Patrick Mulligan.

Simon This used to be a backwater. See that pub over there? Gay men used to go there to fuck in the back room.

May Clearly you're nervous.

Simon No.

May And you're underdressed for the Chop House.

Simon I have to go now, May.

May And the weather's here, so out comes the tattoo. What's that meant to prove?

Simon I've had it for ten years.

May Don't let him get away with it.

Simon I'm off.

May I'm busy myself.

> *Alexander Weekes comes out of the coffee shop.*
> *He's wearing a big, well-worn, old-fashioned, once-*
> *fashionable but now grotesque ladies' summer straw*
> *hat, trimmed with a parrot's head, probably real, and*
> *a peach. He passes straight through. It renders May*
> *practically speechless; gasping for words; she sits*
> *frozen, inert against her will. Simon, standing and*
> *swigging the last of his coffee, doesn't take this in.*

Hat. Hat. Hat.

Simon Goodbye, May.

TWO

Late morning. By the Thames, outside City Hall.
> *Simon is eating a Marks and Spencer sandwich. A Bird*
> *Whistle Seller is selling irritating whistles that create*
> *birdsong. He is twenty-six. He has a backpack and a*
> *guitar in a leather cover nearby. He is demonstrating on*
> *a whistle. He pauses for breath.*

Simon If I buy one, do you quit?

> *The Bird Whistler smiles sadistically and resumes.*

How much?

Bird Whistler A pound. A bargain.

> *The Bird Whistler is Australian. He resumes whistling.*
> *He stops.*

Finished browsing?

Simon Would it be a legal transaction?

Bird Whistler Huh?

Simon Would we be breaking the law? Will you declare this income?

Bird Whistler Shut up, dude. Buy the fucking bird-whistler thingummy or don't buy the fucking bird-whistler thingummy. Carrying on about cash-in-hand, for fuck's sake.

Simon Sorry.

Bird Whistler No problem, dude. So d'you want one? It authentically replicates the song of the common British blackbird, *turdus merula*. One for a pound. Or three for two.

Simon Why would I need three?

Bird Whistler Fine, two for two.

Simon So, how much would four cost?

Bird Whistler One bunch of fives.

Simon Um. Here. Take two for one.

Bird Whistler Oh, thanks, generous, extremely.

They transact. Simon blows his whistle.

Simon You're absolutely right, it really does sound like the song of the *turdus terula*.

Bird Whistler Dude, it's *merula*, not *terula*: if you're gonna take the piss, take it with a bit of style. A bit of wit. Bit of esprit. See you when I see you. Never.

A sound. He looks up involuntarily. Simon does the same. A helicopter. Their eyes follow it. It gets louder and louder. Peculiar shadows. It comes close. The noise is almost unbearable.

Fucking Nora!

It recedes. The noise diminishes, the light adjusts itself. Beat.

Simon So, um, have you been a bird whistler for long?

Beat.

Bird Whistler It's 11.27 in the bloody morning, mate. It's just too much, all right, this outstanding condescension? I haven't even made enough to buy breakfast yet, I don't have to put up with –

Simon Oh, would you like some of my sandwich? Tuna and cucumber.

Bird Whistler No, thank you. Tuna gives me the runs.

Simon Right.

He's stuck with a half-eaten sandwich he no longer wants. The Bird Whistler whistles on another whistle as people pass. No sale.

Bird Whistler Look, if you're after something else, I haven't got it. It's *turdus merula* whistles, or the highway, OK?

Simon My grandmother was Australian.

Beat.

Bird Whistler My grandmother caught a fish this big.

Simon My grandmother was double-jointed.

Bird Whistler Mine swallowed the spider that swallowed the fly.

Simon Mine was a –

Bird Whistler Mine threw dwarfs at the court of King Caractacus.

Beat.

Simon Mine has three lines in *Carry On Regardless*.

Bird Whistler You're joking? No bullshit? Really?

Simon Well, not my grandma, my neighbour. It's true, she really is in *Carry On Regardless*.

Bird Whistler Cool.

Simon She didn't do much else, never made it. She was in an episode of *Catweazle* in 1970.

Bird Whistler Groovetastic.

He blows his whistle.

Simon How long are you in London?

Bird Whistler Three more months, then I have to go. My working holiday runs out.

Simon Bummer.

Bird Whistler Yeah. So. Unless you can marry me or find someone who can, I'll get back to my bird whistles and you can get back to whatever it is you do when you're not making a complete bozo of yourself in front of total strangers.

He goes to his backpack and squats to get something out. The Waiter passes through. He's wearing a long maroon jacket with a buttonhole in the lapel and a tight T-shirt: on the front are the words 'Just Registered' in big letters. He carries a folded Evening Standard *with the headline 'Heathrow Closed'. One hand is clasped to his forehead, over an eye, as if to stop bleeding. Tied to one of his legs is a string daisy-chain of old tin cans, as per the honeymoon-car tradition. He's walking at a pace. Simon clocks him. Inevitably, farcically, they get in each other's way: left, right, left. By the time the Bird Whistler stands with a bottle of water from his backpack, he can only see the Waiter's back.*

Simon I. Sorry. Um. Sorry.

The Waiter smiles like a waiter and exits.

Bird Whistler Dude.

He drinks.

That nutter trod on your toes. You went left first and cleared a path for him. He followed you: he turned his nose up at the path you'd politely made available. That's like friendly fire, mate – and you said sorry. Doesn't add up.

Simon I think I know him, that's all.

Bird Whistler Dude?

Simon Yeah?

Bird Whistler City Hall is my patch. I'm sort of wondering if you wouldn't mind buggering off? No offence, but you kind of drip despondency and you're sort of scaring off my clientele.

Simon Sorry.

Bird Whistler I don't want apologies, mate, I just want you to realise we've had the sale and there's sort of no more need for us to function together any more?

Simon Um. I have to buy a new suit.

Beat.

There's a shop in Hay's Galleria . . . and . . . I need someone to go yes or no. I'd ring a mate but everyone's working. If you could just tell me whether it fits? I'll buy you a beer. Or lunch. Except I'm meeting one of my old, um, teachers for lunch at the Chop House so it can't be lunch. That's why I need the suit, actually, to look, um, prosperous. Could you?

Bird Whistler When you're travelling, you have to be up for everything. Some travellers aren't, I've got no time for it. You have to say yes to every crazy damn thing, 'cause then you'll have stuff to tell your grandkids: anecdotes about large fish and very large fish. Otherwise what's the point? It's a big world.

Beat.

Nup.

Simon No?

Bird Whistler Nup.

Simon It's quite important I look right.

Bird Whistler Bye, dude.

Simon I understand.

The Bird Whistler whistles.

Bird Whistler A pound. Only a pound.

THREE

Lunch. An outdoor table at a restaurant by Tower Bridge.
Simon has just arrived at Patrick's table. Patrick is older than Simon. He's wearing an open-necked, patterned designer shirt. He has a black briefcase under the table. Simon's wearing a new suit; it's not expensive and is slightly too small, though not ridiculously so. He's carrying a Next bag containing the clothes he was wearing earlier. There's a gift on the table wrapped in distinctive paper. A bottle of champagne is chilling in an ice-bucket.

Simon Hi.

Patrick Hi.

Patrick is Irish. Beat.

Simon You haven't changed at all, Patrick.

Patrick Simon?

Simon nods. They shake hands. Beat.

Simon Something the matter?

Patrick No.

Simon Eighteen years, nearly.

Patrick Yes.

Simon Incredible to get your call. I was so . . . I was thrilled.

Patrick I'm sorry, I think there's – I don't –

Simon Simon Gilliver.

Patrick Yes. That's who I'm expecting.

Simon Me.

Patrick I spoke to Simon Gilliver. I got his number from Josh Allen.

Simon You spoke to me.

Patrick ?

Simon I still don't really know how Josh Allen had my number, I haven't seen him for years, but I'm glad he did. Patrick Mulligan. Wow. Bolt from the blue.

Beat.

We spoke.

Patrick I know, I recognise the voice.

Simon You rang me from South Carolina.

Patrick North.

Simon We arranged lunch. Twelve-thirty at the Chop House, booking in your name. Here. As planned.

Patrick Yes.

Beat.

Simon *A Midsummer Night's Dream*, Patrick. Drama summer school, 1987.

Patrick I know, but – Lysander?

Beat.

Simon Puck.

Patrick Puck?

Simon I played Puck. Simon Gilliver. I played Puck.

Patrick Oh. Simon Gilliver played Puck? No.

Simon Yes.

Patrick Simon Gilliver played Lysander.

Simon No, Johnny Hepple played Lysander.

Patrick Johnny Hepple?

Simon Yeah. Johnny Hepple. Jonathan Hepple, QC, now, actually.

Patrick Johnny Hepple. Fuck me. Yes. Simon Gilliver.

Simon Is me. Puck. I couldn't say whether Josh Allen has Johnny Hepple's number. But if you're after Lysander, you're after him. If you're after Puck, you're after me.

Beat.

This isn't what you were expecting.

Patrick Not quite, no. God. OK. Cock up. Yes. Not to worry. Doesn't matter. Have a seat.

Simon You thought you were talking to someone else.

Patrick Yes.

Simon You don't remember me?

Patrick When we spoke, I had Lysander in mind. I thought Simon Gilliver played Lysander. And Josh Allen had Simon Gilliver's number and I rang because I had some fun with Lysander, a laugh. I remember. It's my first trip to London for years, I wanted to make contact with him and –

Beat.

Cock up.

Simon You wouldn't have called if you'd realised.

Patrick It's flooding back. Yes. I see. Fuck. Puck.

Simon It *is* flooding back.

Patrick Champagne?

He hurriedly pours Simon a glass.

Cheers.

Simon Up mine.

Patrick hands him the menu, open.

Patrick Choose. I'm having the steak and kidney pudding. I was going to have the beef, but I've plumped for the steak and kidney.

Simon Quicker.

Patrick Right.

Simon Starter?

Patrick I don't think so.

Simon I don't either.

Patrick Decided?

Simon Oh, yes.

Patrick Excellent.

He gestures, off, then drinks a whole glass. Beat.

I'd forgotten how slow London waiters are.

Beat.

So – Johnny Hepple's a QC?

Simon Me? I'm a senior IT technical support analyst for a property consultant just behind Tate Modern. Been with them since I was twenty-four. Eight years.

Beat.

Patrick Hmn.

He looks towards the river.

Ladies. Doing callisthenics.

The Waiter approaches, now dressed formally in the Chop House uniform (tie and waistcoat). He has a plaster above one eyebrow.

Ah.

Simon clocks the Waiter with surprise.

Waiter Are you ready to order, sir?

Patrick Yes, a bottle of the Château Montus and the steak and kidney pudding.

Waiter With or without oysters, sir?

Patrick Without.

Taking in the Waiter's good-looking face, he changes his mind.

With. That's it, thank you.

Waiter (*to Simon*) Sir?

Simon Um. Um. (*To Patrick*) 'Callisthenics'? (*To the Waiter*) Um. Sirloin steak and chips. And my tomato and mozzarella panini.

Waiter ?

Simon Only if it's ready.

Waiter (*confused*) You want the sirloin, sir?

Simon Yes, please.

Waiter How would you like it done?

Patrick (*to the Waiter, flirtatiously*) Why, what do you want to do with it?

Simon ?

Patrick (*and again*) I'm intrigued by the accent.

   The Waiter smiles politely at Patrick. To Simon:

Waiter Sir?

Simon (*to Patrick*) Are you joking?

Patrick (*to Simon*) Answer the man.

Waiter Sir?

Simon Um. Rare. Medium. Medium-rare.

Waiter Thank you.

Patrick Thank *you*.

Simon Wait – before you go. How many jobs have you got?

Waiter Excuse me, sir?

Simon I'm. You know. I'm still waiting for my tomato and mozzarella panini.

Waiter Mozzarella – ?

Simon The coffee shop, Tooley Street? You said you'd bring it out. I was sitting at the table by the – Quite close to the old woman with the –

Waiter Oh yes, sir. I didn't recognise you. You were wearing a Cockfighter of Bermondsey T-shirt?

Simon No.

Waiter You weren't?

Simon I mean, yes. I've changed.

Beat.

Waiter Two jobs, sir.

Patrick Busy lad.

Waiter Someone didn't turn up at the café. And I wasn't going to do this shift, but –

He stops himself. He tops up their champagne glasses, nods politely, and leaves.

Simon Isn't that funny?

Patrick Yeah.

Simon Tooley Street, I was there this morning, I'm there every morning.

Patrick And you're still waiting for your panini, and you ordered steak and chips. You remind me of my daughter, she'd order a cheeseburger at the Ritz.

Simon It is on the menu. I'd never order something that wasn't.

Beat.

Anyway, you said, 'What do you want to do with it?' when he asked how I wanted it done. So if anyone's being, I don't know, puerile –

Patrick Aren't you a vegetarian?

Simon Oh good, you remember a detail.

Patrick Am I right?

Simon I was when I was a teenager, yes. Not now.

Beat.

I also recently sprayed pesticide on my window boxes and straitjacketed the ladybirds.

Beat.

Do you find London changed?

Patrick Yes.

Beat.

Simon How?

Patrick City Hall, that wasn't there. We took a look this morning. Twice, actually. It's grotty from the outside and it's like this weird, glassy pod when you go in.

Simon I saw the Deputy Mayor earlier.

Beat.

In America ladybirds are called ladybugs.

Beat.

Have you noticed that, where you live in North Carolina?

Patrick smiles uninterestedly and drinks. The Waiter arrives with the wine. He opens it. Patrick places his hand on the Waiter's, perhaps in order to touch the Waiter's hand, certainly to get a full glass and speed things up by avoiding the tasting.

Patrick I'm sure it'll be fine.

The Waiter fills Patrick's glass, then Simon's, and leaves. Patrick drinks. Simon sneezes. He searches for a tissue: the napkin looks too well-laundered to soil with snot. He reaches down into his Next bag and finds, surreptitiously, a plastic packet of brand-new handkerchiefs. He takes one out. He sits up and blows his nose.

Look at that. A hanky.

Simon Um, yeah?

Patrick Something else about the States. No one under the age of seventy-five has a handkerchief. Kleenex all the way.

Simon Oh, it's just that, um, earlier I bought a new suit. Just by Potters Fields there's, um, a Next. I had some time, so I bought one. And hankies, on sale. Tartan ones.

Patrick You're wearing a new suit?

Simon Yeah.

Patrick For me?

Simon No.

Patrick You live nearby?

Simon Yeah.

Patrick Don't you have other suits?

Simon I do, but annoyingly this old thing who's in my life a bit too much said my last one was too big, and suddenly I had this fucked-up need to buy a new one and now I'm stuck with a really money-saving suit from Next. At least it fits.

Patrick (*looking around*) I was hoping to see someone famous.

Simon Next. Then again, I used to shop there. And I still eat at this Indian off Snowsfields I went to when I was skint. I regularly cut myself shaving – and I'm a real bleeder. I still sweat at parties. I'm earning a packet, I could afford Armani, I shop at Next –

Patrick Julie Christie, anyone.

Simon I just don't change.

Patrick Your suit doesn't fit, it's too small.

Simon Is your hotel nearby?

Patrick Why?

Simon I just wondered.

Patrick We'll just have lunch.

Simon Well, of course we'll just have lunch – I was only asking where you were staying.

Patrick St Katharine Docks.

Simon The Thistle Tower?

Patrick With Toni, my wife.

Simon Oh. Where's she today?

Patrick Hornsey.

Simon Hornsey? What's there?

Patrick She's on a walking tour of some sort.

Simon What does she do?

Patrick She's a singer-songwriter.

Simon How long are you here for?

Patrick We leave tomorrow.

Simon You might not get away. I just saw an *Evening Standard* – Heathrow, something about diverted flights? Computer fault.

Patrick Let me get this right. Did you end up being not very good in the *Dream* and, sort of, add lots of words that Shakespeare didn't put there?

Simon It's coming back.

Patrick I remember during rehearsals, you literally growing up in front of us –

Simon Like the plants in May.

Patrick – and you turned out to be this vast galumphing Puck.

Simon Very un-Pucky. Flat-footed and galumphing, you couldn't direct me at all.

Patrick I couldn't direct anyone.

Simon I don't remember that. I remember looking up to you. I thought you were everything. And then you were gone.

Patrick The summer ended.

The Waiter arrives and serves them their meals.

Thank you.

Simon Cheers, you can cancel the panini now.

Waiter The – ?

Simon You know, the – Drop it. Really.

The Waiter nods and leaves.

Polish, you know. *Bon appétit.*

Patrick Yes.

They eat. Simon nods at the gift.

Simon What's that?

Patrick A gift.

Simon Who for?

Patrick Simon Gilliver.

Simon Me.

Patrick half-shrugs.

What is it?

Patrick It's a biography. Of Brando. I wrote it.

Simon No way? Brando? Fuck, that's impressive. Did you really? I didn't know that.

Patrick It wasn't picked up here.

Simon Oh.

Patrick I don't know why.

Simon So it was published in America?

Patrick Hong Kong.

Simon You're big in Hong Kong? Wow. How *Spinal Tap*.

Patrick You're the second person to say that to me today.

Simon No, I don't mean to be rude: it's really stunning.

He picks something out of his mouth and uses his fork to play with his food.

Patrick All right?

Simon No. I have . . . raw meat on my plate.

Patrick Raw or rare?

Simon Oh, it's raw. I know the difference.

Patrick Get the waiter, complain.

Simon It's all right, I'll just, um, eat the chips.

Patrick What are you talking about? That's revolting. Get the waiter.

Simon The vegetables are lovely.

Patrick On a bed of blood?

Simon It's not bleeding, it's just raw.

Patrick I'm calling the waiter.

Simon Could we swap meals?

Patrick Simon Gilliver, Simon Gilliver: you were so placid and nice, not like ordinary kids at that age, so polite and good.

Simon It's why you cast me as Puck.

Patrick Puck isn't nice.

Simon But niceness is boyish.

Patrick Get the waiter.

Simon I can't. I hate – I don't like this sort of thing. Bollocks, I don't even *eat* – Why did I order a sodding – And today. I just think there's enough on my plate already, like what the hell I'm even doing here?

Patrick It's an accident, Simon.

Simon Yes, because you're a fucking idiot.

Patrick It was an honest mistake.

Simon How old are you now, Patrick?

Patrick Thirty-eight.

The Waiter approaches.

Waiter Is everything all right?

Simon No. Um.

Waiter Oh?

Simon You see. Um. If you ask that question, you have to be, um, prepared for more than one response. 'Oh?'

with that fillip of surprise, 'No is the wrong answer, *duhhh*,' is really irritating. Please don't ask, 'Is everything all right?' then act surprised if people say 'No.'

Patrick You said, 'No um.'

Simon What?

Patrick You said 'No. Um.' He said, 'Is everything all right?' and you answered, 'No. Um.' There was an 'um' on the end of it. I remember that um.

> On the ground um
> Sleep sound.
> I'll um apply
> To your eye, um
> Gentle lover, um remedy.

Waiter *Twelfth Night*?

Patrick No, the *Dream*.

Waiter Oh, of course, that's right, yeah.

Simon Hellooo?

Patrick His meat is apparently raw um.

Waiter It's rare, sir, you asked for it rare.

Simon Did I?

Waiter Yes.

Simon It's not rare. It's raw.

Patrick It really is raw, I can um vouch for it.

Simon You know something about the planes, don't you? I think? Because –

Waiter ?

Simon I'm wondering could you tell us, have they been grounded? My friend's only in town for a couple of days –

we never should have met, it's very pastoral-lyrical – so, if there are no flights, that'd be fortunate because then he'll have the time to see all the others.

Waiter We're waiting for our head chef, his Brussels flight was re-routed to Manchester. That's all I know.

Simon Your head chef?

Waiter Yes, sir. I'll deal with this problem straight away, of course.

He picks up Simon's plate.

Simon It's amazing how in one job you're a surly cunt and in the other you're a surly sophisticated faux-French cunt. And bad fucking form to tell me the head chef hasn't even bothered to show up. *You've served me an open wound.*

Beat.

Patrick Please. I'm sorry. My friend is sorry.

Waiter I'll take this to the sous-chef, sir. Many apologies.

Patrick Thank you.

Waiter Yes, sir.

Patrick I love your Polish accent.

Waiter My er –? Thanks.

Patrick Where in Poland?

Waiter Krakow.

Patrick Oh, how lovely, that's a beautiful place.

Waiter Thanks.

Patrick Thank you.

Waiter I'll be back in a moment.

Patrick We're very sorry.

The Waiter takes the plate off.

Sweet.

Simon Pardon?

Patrick Sweet of him.

Simon Have you been to Krakow?

Patrick No.

Simon How do you know it's a beautiful place?

Patrick I've heard.

Simon I went to Krakow last May.

Patrick Is it a beautiful place?

Simon Yes.

Patrick There you go then.

Simon What would you have said if he was from Warsaw? Warsaw's not beautiful. They bombed the knickers off it then the Reds got creative on the rubble. Lucky he's not from Warsaw. Please don't talk to the waiter, Patrick, this is my problem.

Patrick You have to calm down, Simon. I made an honest mistake. We can have a nice lunch, then go our separate ways. All right?

The Waiter returns.

Waiter Christophe, the sous-chef, is very sorry, sir. Our steaks are seared first. A seared but uncooked steak got muddled with the cooked ones. We'll deduct it. Would you like another bottle of champagne on the house?

Simon No, thank you.

Patrick Yes, please.

Waiter (*to Patrick*) Allow me to take your meal and we'll start again.

Patrick No, I'm fine. He'll wait.

Waiter If you're sure?

Patrick How long's your shift?

Waiter I finish at four, sir.

He exits. Patrick tucks into his steak and kidney pudding. Beat.

Simon
On the ground
Sleep sound.

Patrick eats.

I fucked that up. During interval I felt so crap. I'd sounded sort of squeaky, and Lysander – Johnny Hepple – had tried to put me off by doing a shagging thing with his thumb and forefinger.

Patrick And you made all those interjections. Incredible how an extra syllable can decimate metre.

Jack shall have Jill um;
Naught shall go um ill er.

The Waiter arrives with champagne. Patrick simply swipes the bottle and opens it himself. He pours a glass and the Waiter exits.

Simon I knew I'd fucked it up and that you'd be disappointed in me. I never understood how to say it. Anyway, I was having a piss. I saw you in the mirror. You came up behind me. You'd been drinking. You took my cock, held it, sprayed it, nuzzled my neck.

Patrick I remember you fucking up the scene. I remember Lysander trying to make you laugh. I saw it all from the follow-spot.

Simon Then you took me into a cubicle and fucked me.

Patrick I remember you instigating that.

Simon No.

Patrick Oh, yes.

Simon I just find it so interesting that you've, um, miscomputed my name, so badly.

Patrick What are you on about, Simon, a mirror? A mirror above a urinal, what, what, what are you on about, what mirror?

Simon ?

Patrick Are you comfortable in your skin?

Simon Yes.

Patrick Are you gay?

Simon Yes.

Patrick How many people have you slept with in the eighteen years since the *Dream*?

Simon ?

Patrick Lost count?

Simon Of course.

Patrick So what's the problem?

Simon There isn't a problem, except that you were older.

Patrick How old are you now?

Simon Thirty-two.

Patrick And I'm only thirty-eight.

Simon You were twenty.

Patrick Come on, Simon. I was a child then, a kid. And you, a gay man, making something of another man touching you?

Simon Is thirty-two too old now?

Patrick What are you talking about?

Simon Are you really attracted to that random Krakowian waiter or are you just scared witless of what I'm saying to you?

Patrick Don't be an idiot.

Simon I know where Jonathan Hepple, QC, works, by the way: I assume you assumed you'd get a fuck out of him. He's bald and lives on a houseboat.

Patrick You know, I could travel the States and I wouldn't find steak and kidney pudding like this. But I'm bringing this to a close.

Simon We don't forget our teachers. And I remember.

Patrick I wasn't your teacher. I was a volunteer director on a drama summer school.

He gestures, 'The bill,' off.

I remember you. You went 'um' a lot, but you were an independent little so-and-so. This isn't what you're trying to make it out to be. It doesn't fit. You were a precious little fucker who knew exactly what he was up to. Because you're gay and gay children know. They're operators. Hunters. They're very evolved, very sophisticated. They have to be. I remember. And you're still the same. Even in a cheap suit. This isn't you. You don't care. You're too clever and tough for this damage bullshit. If you're a fuck-up, don't look here. Now drink up, Puck. All is ended.

He mops his head with his napkin. He gets up and strides off. He turns back immediately to pick up his black briefcase, irritated that he forgot it, defensive that he feels the need to take it, and exits. Simon is on his own. His breathing is heavy and measured. He stares at nothingness for some time. He drinks: his hand shakes. The Waiter arrives with the bill.

Waiter The sous-chef is . . .

He runs out of words and gestures feebly towards the kitchen. He leaves. Patrick returns, having splashed his face with water. He sits and self-consciously runs his hand through a wet section of his fringe. He forks some steak and kidney pudding and is about to eat.

Simon My neighbour told me to poison your lunch.

Patrick You've never spoken to anyone about this, have you, Simon?

Simon Then again, she's out to lunch.

Patrick Because there's nothing.

Simon Can I have the Brando book?

Patrick Order it from Amazon.

Beat.

Simon Would that be Amazon dot co dot hongkong, or –

Patrick thumps his fist on the table, suppressed rage. Beat.

My neighbour's an actress. Every week she's reading a new biography of some obscure woman she thinks is going to be the subject of a biographical film she's going to star in. Often they're related to someone more famous.

Clara Schumann. Clementine Churchill. This week it was Eleanor Marx who was Karl Marx's daughter. The sad thing is, I've realised, today, that we're on a merry-go-round. Just this morning I had déjà vu: we've had Eleanor Marx before. Twice, maybe. She's going round in circles. It's that delusional.

Patrick Eleanor Marx was tricked into killing herself by her husband.

Simon Really? How?

Patrick He made a suicide pact with her then reneged on it.

Simon Bastard.

Patrick No one cares about Marxes any more.

Simon How old was she?

Patrick (*shrugging*) Forties.

He notices the bill and picks it up.

Simon May Gradner must be ninety.

Patrick May Gradner?

Simon nods.

I know who May Gradner is.

Simon You don't.

Patrick Of course I do, she's got a tiny role in *The Nightcomers*. And she's in a *Carry On*. Plays a nurse. But it's not *Nurse. Regardless*?

Simon You don't know that.

Patrick Check IMDb.

Simon I mean, I know that, you don't know that.

Patrick You live next door to May Gradner?

Simon Yeah.

Patrick That's amazing. I'd love to interview her. God, she must have a leg in the grave. Isn't she South African?

Simon Patrick. Nobody except for the happiest pansy this side of Mount Are-You-Being-Served could know who May Gradner is. And to know she was Second Nurse in *Carry On Regardless* takes a uniquely closeted kind of grand-old-lady-collecting fruitiness.

The Waiter arrives.

Patrick We've finished here.

Waiter The sous-chef would like to know if –

Patrick My colleague has to leave.

Beat.

Waiter Very good, sir.

Patrick I'm sorry. Thank you. Wait, take my card.

He puts his briefcase on the table, opens it via a combination lock and slips his hand in for his wallet. Simon bends under the table immediately to fumble through his Next bag for cash.

(*To the Waiter*) What happened to your –? (*He indicates his eyebrow.*)

Simon is under the table, and the Waiter takes the opportunity to indicate he's fed up with the come-on.

Waiter Well, sir, I had the shit kicked out of me. By my fiancée.

Patrick Fiancée?

Waiter Someone with authority who'd condemn that kind of thing in public. And on top of everything else now I'm stuck with her appellation injected into my skin for eternity.

This leaves Patrick nonplussed. Simon sits up and slams some notes down.

Simon I like to pay for my own raw meat when I can. (*To the Waiter*) I don't need change.

The Waiter picks up the money and exits. Patrick looks to Simon.

Patrick Simon.

He holds out his hand. Simon shakes it.

I'm very sorry I thought you were someone else. But it's been good to catch up. You were a very good Puck.

Simon Thank you, Patrick. You weren't.

Patrick Good luck.

A glass smashes, off. Patrick looks behind him.

Simon Very clumsy, the Poles. Oh look, and he's down on his knees already.

Beat.

Good luck with your Brando biography.

He nods to the gift.

Please. May I?

Patrick shrugs and drinks. Simon picks it up and unwraps it.

Look at that. *Brando: a Life*, by Patrick Mulligan.

Patrick Goodbye.

Simon And you've inscribed it. 'To Simon. My old Lysander. Patrick.'

Patrick Goodbye.

Simon How sweet.

FOUR

Mid-afternoon. A park, Potters Fields, near City Hall.
A tree, a bin, a bench. Bird song from the Bird
Whistler wafts through the air. A Woman in dark
sunglasses is watching Simon from a distance. She is
thirty-six. She has thick, dyed-red hair in dreadlocks,
pulled back from her face. She is wearing a short skirt.
She is thin. Her right hand is a prosthetic. In one hand
Simon is holding a fake purple-white flower; in the other,
his mobile phone. He stares at the flower as he speaks.

Simon May? May, I'm in trouble. Um. I've lost my keys.
I've got no idea where . . . I think they must have fallen
out when I . . . forget it. As soon as you get this, ring me
on my mobile – I need to drop by to pick up the spare
set. Er . . . thanks. I suppose I'll have to . . . um. Bye. (*He
hangs up. To himself*) Crap.

> *For a second he could hit something. He searches in*
> *the Next bag, losing the flower to the grass. Fed up, he*
> *decides to get out of the suit and back into his clothes*
> *from earlier: he finds the tree behind which to do this.*
> *The Woman observes until her curiosity gets the better*
> *of her. She approaches him in flagrante delicto.*

Woman What are you doing?

The Woman is American.

Simon Go away. Please go away. (*He continues changing.*)

Woman There are children in this park.

Simon Shut up, bitch, it's a school day. (*He is surprised
by his own vehemence.*) I'm sorry. I didn't mean to call
you bitch.

Woman Oh, I can be a bitch, bastard. What's your name?

Simon What?

Woman Where do you come from?

Simon What do you want?

Woman Who are you?

Simon Why should I tell you?

Woman God help me, I'll get you arrested: what's your name, freak?

Simon is out of the suit. He pulls on his Cockfighter of Bermondsey T-shirt, and he is dressed.

Simon I didn't expose myself to anyone, child or otherwise. I'm not interested in children, children suck. So why don't you just piss off?

Woman Patrick Mulligan is my husband.

Beat.

Simon You're following me?

Toni Name.

Beat.

Simon Simon.

Toni Simon what?

Simon Simon Gilliver.

Toni Simon Gilliver?

Simon I have to get my locks changed.

Toni I've never heard of any Simon Gilliver. Patrick's diary doesn't mention any Simon Gilliver.

Simon I haven't seen Patrick since Kajagoogoo had their hit.

Toni You just had lunch with him, you lying son of a bastard.

Simon Why are you following me?

Toni Because I followed him. To the Chop Shop. You came out. I thought, ploy: I was on your ass. Have I lost him, Gulliver? Why have I been walking in a circle for quarter of an hour?

Simon I can't find my keys. I've been looking for a place to get out of the suit.

Toni Well, it's a bad suit.

Simon Shut up, no it's not.

Toni He said he was meeting a publisher.

Simon He lied.

Toni No, you don't look literary.

Simon Why not? – Yes I do.

Toni Where are you rendezvous-ing? At a hotel?

Simon I never want to see him again.

Toni grabs the fake flower from the grass.

Toni I know you've stolen this. I know it doesn't belong to you. (*She clips it in her hair aggressively. It looks rather lovely.*) Don't fuck with me.

Simon You followed the wrong mug. You should have stuck with him. Now leave me alone.

The Bird Whistler passes. He has packed up: he's carrying his backpack and guitar.

Wait! Bird Whistler! Bruce, my man!

Bird Whistler (*to himself*) Oh, bloody hell.

Simon Hold on!

Bird Whistler Hi, dude.

Simon (*sotto voce*) Keep walking.

Bird Whistler How was your lunch?

Simon I said, keep walking.

Bird Whistler (*ignoring this; nodding at the Next bag*) You bought your suit, then?

Toni (*to the Bird Whistler*) You know this man? Is his name Simon Gulliver?

Simon Gilliver.

Bird Whistler Don't know him from Adam, babes.

He half-recognises her.

Hello? Earlier? The incident? You were checking the view? Inside –

Toni Are you fucking my husband as well?

Bird Whistler Huh?

Simon I didn't fuck your husband, your husband fucked me. Bareback, with nothing but spit, and it hurt. It was my first time. It was between acts three and four of a summer school production of one of Shakespeare's fine comedies, over a loo that needed a good scrub, in a church hall in Bromley, on a Sunday in August 1987.

This renders Toni silent.

Toni That's further back than I was expecting.

Beat.

Bird Whistler Double-breasted or single?

Simon Single.

Bird Whistler Most wise.

Simon It's too small for me.

He stuffs the Next bag and its contents into the bin.

Bird Whistler You did need my help?

Simon It was a lot to ask.

Bird Whistler I reckon, dude.

Toni Would you mind if I sat down?

Bird Whistler Free-ish country.

Toni Thank you.

She sits on one end of the park bench. Beat.

Bird Whistler (*to Simon*) I didn't want to be rude, but it's an intimate thing.

Simon I understand. I'd have said no in your position.

Beat.

Toni How old are you, Simon?

Simon Thirty-two.

Beat.

Bird Whistler OK. I've gotta make tracks.

Simon Wait. I'm glad we bumped into each other. I've been thinking. I could help you.

Bird Whistler I get the feeling your help might be a hindrance on the whole, dude.

Simon Someone's just moved out; I'm looking for a flatmate. And anyone can get hitched now, and I'm really keen to screw this particular Home Secretary, so we could fake a tenancy agreement, photoshop some holiday snaps.

Bird Whistler You and me?

Simon Yeah.

Bird Whistler Oh listen, thanks, mate, that's really nice and stuff. But firstly I'm not gay and two I'm really quite law-abiding and c) I think you, like, let too many cricket balls fly straight through to the stumps. We'd never get on domestically.

Toni Where are you from?

Bird Whistler Adelaide.

Toni Is that your guitar?

Bird Whistler Absolutely, dude.

Toni You're a busker?

Bird Whistler I eat fire, I juggle, I stand really still. But are you interested in buying a nifty whistle that imitates the song of the British blackbird? They're Very Easy to Play. (*He takes one out of his pocket and blows it.*) One pound fifty.

Toni I'm interested in buying a gun so I can shoot my cheating husband in the lunchbox.

Bird Whistler Too indiscreet, babes, your operation's already too uncontained.

Beat.

Anyone want an ice cream?

Simon Strawberry Magnum.

Toni Something orange.

Bird Whistler Watch my gear?

Simon nods. The Bird Whistler piles up his backpack and guitar next to the bench. He puts the bird whistle

42

*on top. He exits. Simon sits on the other end of the
bench. Beat.*

Simon Is your name Toni?

Toni He talks about me?

Simon Toni, I don't know what you want from me. But it
wasn't even me Patrick wanted to see today. He thought
'Simon Gilliver' was someone else. Johnny Hepple, his
Lysander. He wanted to meet that boy, not me, not Puck.
He hasn't thought about this Simon Gilliver for eighteen
years.

   Beat.

Nothing happened. Not even lunch. My food was raw.

Toni Where did he go?

Simon I don't know, Toni.

Toni You were fourteen?

Simon Yes.

   Beat.

I don't know what he was expecting. If he fucked Johnny
Hepple he must've been confident Johnny Hepple wasn't
going to mind that now.

   Beat.

But Johnny Hepple wasn't a kid, he was eighteen.

   Beat.

Anyway. I was a shock.

Toni Did you know what you were doing?

Simon I don't know.

Toni He's not into kids.

43

Simon I was fourteen.

Toni I know everything about Patrick now, I've got his number, it's not children, it's men, men. You think he's a paedophile?

Simon No, but –

Toni Was it against your will?

Simon I don't know.

Toni Because you are gay, right?

This angers Simon.

Simon Yeah.

Toni And when did you become gay?

Simon You've just done exactly what he did.

Toni But are you scarred by it?

Beat.

Simon Not until he rang me.

Beat.

I . . . today, I . . .

Beat.

Toni My husband is something else. What makes a man tick that way? I almost wonder if he's a monster. But he's not *that* kind . . . I'm sorry, Simon Gilliver, I've enough to deal with, I can't add in horny teenagers.

Beat.

Simon The airport's closed. What do you think that means?

Toni It means computer failure.

Simon I don't know.

Toni Don't Fox News me, jackass. It's a computer failure.

Beat.

Simon I don't want anything . . . I wasn't expecting . . . I don't want anything from anyone . . . but to not remember the names, to get them muddled like that, or at least to have miscomputed me. That must mean something. Consciously not logging names: guilt.

Toni Too many names to log: promiscuity. Agitate the unfaithful bone, it jigs away like Jolson. The first affair is always the start of a list. Cheats explain it away as 'only sex'. Sex is never 'only', it doesn't live by itself and breathe its own special air. 'Only sex': the self-justifying mantra of chicken-shits. I come with him to London for a vacation, and he still can't keep his goddamn paws off people. This morning was beautiful. New things, all around. I really didn't expect Patrick to disappear. I really thought he would step out of our hotel, come to Waterloo Station and go on the goddamn Kinks Walking Tour with me. Where the fuck is he?

Simon Whoever you're after doesn't include me. You could try Jonathan Hepple, QC. But I think it's a certain Eastern European waiter you really need.

Toni A waiter?

Simon From the Chop House.

Toni Oh, for God's sake.

She gets her mobile phone out. She gets up a number and holds it up to Simon.

Call him. Arrange to meet.

Simon No.

Toni Threaten him with the cops.

Simon Don't do this to me.

Toni I want to catch this bastard at it, Simon. You can find out for me. Do it on your own cell. I've got a child, you piece of shit.

Beat. Reading the number from Toni's phone, Simon dials on his own.

Simon Hello? – Patrick, it's Simon: you know, '87, Thatcher back in, you gob in my arse? – Hmn? – Oh, hello, I'm the raw-steak man, *you* gobbed in my coffee this morning and I'm still waiting for that panini?

Toni Who is it?

Simon What's your name again, pan?

Toni ?

Simon He says his name's Aurek. Aurek the waiter. Follow *this* voice.

Toni grabs the phone.

Toni Give me my husband, bastard!

She grabs the bird whistle from the top of the backpack and blows it hard down the line. Simon takes back his phone and hangs up.

He slips away from me like a fucking salamander.

Silence. Unexpectedly Simon starts to cry, to sob. It's embarrassing to him. He recovers.

Simon.

Simon Yes?

Toni I have one hand.

Simon I see that.

Toni Whatever the matter is, it can't be worse than having only one hand.

Simon ?

Toni I mean it.

Simon You have the monopoly on pain?

Toni I don't have much patience for people and their little predicaments. Most of you have two hands. If your flight's cancelled, you're fired, there's a black hair in your spaghetti – you've all got two hands. So you're all really lucky when you think about it. Most of you seem egotistical to me.

Simon There's no seems about it, we are.

Toni I would rather encounter campylobacter in myself than self-centredness in others.

Simon Me too.

Toni Campylobacter is a form of severe food-poisoning, Simon.

Simon I know.

Toni I was a guitarist. With a contract. I was signed by the label that signed the Melvins, there are six hundred copies of a four-track EP pressed on orange vinyl. Five drug-fucked ex-moshers in Seattle still know who I am. The point is, Simon: whatever your problem is, it isn't as big as mine.

Beat. Simon wipes his eyes. Toni produces an old, thin-leather prize-fighter's boxing glove from her shoulder-bag.

Simon What's that?

Toni Marlon Brando's boxing glove.

Simon ?

Toni A discarded souvenir from *On the Waterfront*, a picture from 1954 by Elia Kazan about corruption and gangsterism in unions, with a really great score by Lenny Bernstein, my favourite conductor and another no-good bisexual piece of ass-chasing plankton.

Simon Marlon Brando's boxing glove?

Toni Yeah.

Simon Here, in Potters Fields?

Toni Why the hell not? It's a world-class spot.

Beat.

Simon Is it real?

Toni Of course.

Simon I don't believe you.

Toni I don't care.

Simon Whose is it? Aside from Marlon Brando's?

Toni Patrick's. I stole it.

Simon Patrick owns Brando's boxing glove?

Toni His prize possession. Christie's auction. He loves it more than his daughter. He adores it. He guards it like those freakos who collect Nazi china.

Simon Why don't you just leave?

Toni Let's see. My daughter. My hand. My money. Ten years down the dumper. Fuck him. Men? Fuck him.

Simon Can I touch it?

Toni No.

Simon Please.

Toni No.

Simon I think I deserve it. I'd like to have it.

Toni Out of the question. I was unbelievably lucky to get it. He keeps it hidden, locked in a portable purse of decadence. He doesn't even know I know about it. I spied on him whispering sweet nothings to it late one evening when he thought I was asleep. He slipped up, let the purse out of his sight, I cracked the code. It wasn't pretty, getting this thing out: I had to claw my way through Jackie Onassis memorabilia, I broke my fingernail on Mae West's enema bag, I was so deep into the eccentric-fairy-closet I was half expecting to find a lion, a witch and Condoleezza Rice, then there it was. I deserve this thing. Everything I've been through. Tribulations like you wouldn't believe. You couldn't fathom them if you tried.

Simon (*suddenly irritated*) Did he fuck you when you were a pubescent?

Toni Don't you claim my trauma.

Simon So you only have one hand? Boo-hoo-hoo. Find me a cross, we'll chop one half off and nail you to it –

Toni My hand was crushed changing a car tyre outside Raleigh-Durham airport because of a jack Patrick didn't assemble properly.

Simon – and you'd never get a hair in your spaghetti bolognese because you clearly don't touch spaghetti, Atkins-carcass: what did he see in you, sitting there like some eviscerated paper-clip, for fuck's sake eat, human beings need food, you silly diaphanous ant.

Toni shoves her hand into the boxing glove and punches Simon in the face.

Toni You got me on a bad day.

Simon Ouch.

Toni A contender, moi? – Oh, yes.

Simon Ouch.

He puts his hand to his eye. The Bird Whistler enters with two Magnums and an orange lolly.

Bird Whistler Here we are, dudes. Shit, man, are you all right?

Simon Yes. Everything's fine. Really.

Bird Whistler You sure?

Simon Absolutely. Ouch.

Bird Whistler What happened?

Simon Give me that, I'm starving.

Toni It wasn't that hard.

Bird Whistler No strawberry. White or Classic?

Simon Classic.

The Bird Whistler unwraps a Magnum and gives it to Simon.

Bird Whistler For you.

Simon Thanks.

He eats it ravenously, one hand still to his eye. The Bird Whistler unwraps the lolly and gives it to Toni.

Bird Whistler For you.

Toni Thanks.

The Bird Whistler sits between them: three on a bench. They eat their ice creams in silence.

Bird Whistler I have first-aid.

Simon shakes his head. They eat.

I hate the sight of pain; you need ice.

He gets a plastic bag out of his backpack and crushes his ice cream into it. He puts it to Simon's eye, patiently and gently.

There, hold. It's gonna be a shiner. All right?

Simon nods. They eat in silence. Simon shares his Magnum with the Bird Whistler.

Toni (*to Simon*) How many numbers have you got in your cell?

Simon Hmn?

Toni Tell me.

Simon I dunno.

Toni How many?

Simon About fifty.

Toni Hah, beat you, I got a hundred and ninety-one.

Simon Are you serious?

They eat in silence.

Toni All gay men are children.

And again.

Simon Here's a word you don't hear very often these days. Callisthenics.

Toni Yes, it does sound old-fashioned.

Simon Patrick used it to describe some women stretching before a jog in front of the Chop House.

Bird Whistler We all have verbal tics. Australians tend to shorten words. Yanks tend to use more than is strictly necessary.

They eat.

Simon He said callisthenics: he is a wanker.

Toni Simon.

Simon Young brisk Aryans down on the seashore, doing their callisthenics.

Toni I'd appreciate it if you didn't call Patrick a 'wanker'. I don't like that British word.

Simon Pardon me?

Toni Please don't be rude about my family.

    Beat.

Simon I must, I must, I must improve my bust.

    Toni rips the flower out of her hair.

Toni If you didn't want anything why do you have this? I know it belongs to him. Why do you share this weird thing? (*To the Bird Whistler*) Are you looking at my tits?

Bird Whistler Are you looking at my tackle?

Toni What's your name?

Bird Whistler Angus.

Toni Angus?

Angus Like the cattle.

Toni Dismal.

Simon And who are you to tell me not to call Patrick a wanker? Patrick is a bona fide, first-class wanker. Don't tell me what I can and can't call him. Your boxing glove's worth diddly-squat, by the way.

Toni It's worth megabucks, it's Marlon Brando's.

Simon (*Michael Caine*) Yeah, and not a lot of people know. That this. Is Michael Caine's watch.

Angus John Denver's guitar, mate.

They share a laugh.

Toni Doesn't matter, I don't want to sell it, I want to pummel Patrick to death with it. I'm going to wait in the hotel till he comes back, then with the hand of Brando I'm going to kill my husband. And I want every man he's ever banged to know it was me and that it was because of them, even if the banging took place before the Big fucking Bang; I'm finally doing it, I swear to God.

She throws the flower irritably into Simon's lap. Beat.

Angus Dude. I've been thinking.

Simon It's a good idea.

Angus No, not that. Can I have the suit? Seems a waste.

Simon Oh. Sure.

Angus looks into the bin and pulls out the Next bag. Something else grabs his attention: he pulls it out. It's a summer hat trimmed with a parrot's head and a peach.

Angus What the –?

Simon stands and silently takes the hat. Angus takes the suit out of the Next bag. He puts on the jacket: it fits.

Smooth.

During this, Simon, with the hat in hand, stands still and very carefully scans the park. Angus stuffs the suit trousers into his backpack, leaving the Next bag on the bench.

Toni That's a very bad suit.

Angus Not in Elephant and Castle it's not.

Toni How long have you played?

Angus All my life.

Toni I used to play.

Angus Really?

Toni And write.

Angus What kind of stuff?

Toni Look at me: folk-rock-grunge – what else?

Angus Could I hear something?

Toni Please don't.

   Beat.

Angus We could play together.

Toni I said please don't.

Angus We could try. It might work.

Toni Let it rest.

   Angus gets his guitar out.

Angus I'll strum. For you. You understand?

Toni No.

Angus Let me sit on your knee.

   Toni looks at him. Beat. Angus sits on her knee.
See?

Toni I don't want to do this.

Angus Comfy?

Toni I'm really not.

Angus Don't stop the music, man. You're fine.

Toni It's been a while.

Angus I can feel it off you, mate. I've never been to Seattle: but you're Seattle aren't you?

Toni half-smiles.

Oh, yeah. You're Seattle. I wanna hear one of yours.

Toni No.

Angus All right? OK?

Toni All right.

Angus OK. What do you want?

Toni Give me a simple 4/4 swing.

So, Angus is sitting on Toni's knee, with the guitar on his knee. He strums, and behind him, with her good hand, Toni fingers the chords. It's uneasy at first, but within seconds their innate musicality shines through.

Feeling it?

Angus Sure, dude. Tandem-jamming.

Toni Swing it. Guh ga-ga, g-guh ga-ga, g-guh ga-ga, OK?

Angus Go for it, babes.

Toni One, two, a-one, two, three, four –

She sings:

Love is like an apple,
Love is like a pear,
Love is like a scented rose:
Sweetness everywhere.

But apples, they turn sour,
Pears rot on the grass,
So shed no tears when roses prick:

That's just love,
Biting your fat –
Vag.

It's somethin' tragical,
Love: it bites you on the –
Snatch.

It's only natural,
Love: it nips you in the –
Bush.

Ain't gonna cushion it,
Love: it likes to chop your –
Grass.

I'm passin' info 'cause
Peaches rot, and
Pricks go blunt, yeah,
Love, it always pulls this stunt,
Girl, love it likes to bite you on the –
If-ever-the-purty-lovin'-starts,
There's-gonna-be-teeth-marks-on-your-parts.

Angus Ha!

Toni Don't stop me now.

They continue playing.

Angus Dude, you're filthy. My turn – 4/4 traditional
shanty, D, D, G-A, G-A, D. Got it?

Toni That's pretty basic, honey, I got it.

Angus Then soup it up! One, two, three, four –

*She rests her neck on his shoulder as she fingers. They
play a traditional shanty, slightly rocked-up.*

In South Australia I was born,
Heave away, haul away;

In South Australia round Cape Horn,
We're bound for South Australia.

Heave away, you rolling king,
Heave away, haul away;
Heave away you'll hear me sing,
We're bound for South Australia.

And as you wallop around Cape Horn,
Heave away, haul away;
You wish to Christ you'd never been born,
We're bound for South Australia.

Heave away you rolling king –

Toni harmonises.

Angus *and* **Toni**
Heave away! Haul away!

Angus
Heave away you'll hear me sing,
We're bound for –

Angus *and* **Toni**
South Australia!

Angus
Way-hey!

Toni laughs and screams.

Toni

Wooh-hooh!

*They beam at each other, then continue jamming.
Simon, still holding the hat, picks up the boxing glove,
slips it and the fake flower into the Next bag and
walks off with them. The lights fade on the guitaring
couple. Simon stops in the distance to look back at
them, then disappears into the trees.*

Act Two

ONE

Morning. The interior of the coffee shop.

Muzak. The Waiter appears from behind the counter, on his mobile phone. He is wearing the Trainee Barista T-shirt. No plaster.

Waiter Hi, I've just started celebrating!

He pops open a bottle of champagne.

I'm round the corner, actually. – Don't panic, I'm covering, I'll be out on time. – Wait.

May enters. She has a book under her arm and her cloth bag over her shoulder: it clearly contains other books. She's wearing the big summer hat trimmed with parrot's head and peach.

May Good morning, a coffee, please. Regular. No frills, an ordinary coffee.

The Waiter is gobsmacked by the hat.

You're looking at my book, aren't you?

She holds it up.

This is a biography of May Morris, daughter of the designer and socialist William, you'll have heard of him. A biographical picture's in the offing. They saw me playing Miss Mountshaft's pedicure in that episode of *The Good Life* and thought I had May's Pre-Raphaelite frame. She modelled for Rossetti.

The Waiter stares at her blankly. She produces another book.

Elizabeth Siddal, Rossetti's wife. Obscured her reputation when she OD'd on laudanum. (*She puts the exact money on the counter.*) For here. I'll wait.

The Waiter makes the coffee.

You're new.

Waiter (*shaking his head*) I don't work this shift.

May Where's Marco?

Waiter Running late.

May Mmn, it's warm. It usually takes me fifteen minutes to walk here but I ran out of breath.

She puts the books in the bag, takes off her hat, puts it on the counter and wipes both cheeks with her hands.

People in hot countries eat hot foods: they know what they're doing. What's your name?

Waiter Aurek.

May Aurek: where's that from?

Aurek Poland.

May You're Polish?

Aurek My name is.

May We've noticed the arrival of the Poles.

Aurek ?

May My neighbour went. He was deeply affected by Auschwitz. Have you been to Auschwitz?

Aurek I'm not – Yes.

He serves her the coffee across the counter.

May Did it profoundly affect you?

Aurek Well. Yeah.

He looks at his watch. He can't contain a smile.

May This is the worst thing I can drink. Bladder cancer, riddled with it. You find that funny?

Aurek hasn't been listening to her.

Aurek I'm getting married today at City Hall.

May Numbskull of a child. Mazel Tov.

She goes outside with her coffee. She forgets about her summer hat. Aurek picks up his mobile.

Aurek Hi. – So Marco owes me? It's money. – No, don't come in: bad luck!

He hangs up. Simon enters, dressed in his Cockfighter of Bermondsey T-shirt.

Simon A large cappuccino and . . . a tomato and mozzarella panini, toasted. In.

Aurek Four eighty-five.

Simon I'll be outside.

Aurek Cool top.

Simon Um . . .

He doesn't know what to say. Aurek gives him his change.

Aurek I'll bring it out.

Simon nods and goes outside. Aurek mutters sarcastically.

Thank you . . . No, no, thank *you* . . .

He raps and throws a few shapes as he works.

Muzak. Muzak. Dig that funky funky café muzak.

He takes some care getting the cappuccino just right.
Gorgeous.

Gorgeous.

He looks about, then gobs in it. He exits with it. The
wall phone rings. Aurek enters, muttering:

'That'll be the phone, dear.' Um, you *think*? (*He answers.*)
Hello, Café . . . Marco, where are you, cunt? If you're
not here in five minutes, I'll – It's my big day, Marco! –
You do that. – Move!

He hangs up. He drinks champagne. His mobile phone
rings. He checks the caller ID. He vacillates but
decides to answer: he blocks his nose and mimics
Alexander.

Aurek's phone? – No, this is Alexander Weekes. – I'm
sorry, Aurek can't make it to the Chop House today, he
er, slipped in the shower, needed stitches above his eye. –
Christophe, sous-chef, got it. – Oh? Why?

His attention is diverted outside.

Fucking hell! (*On the phone:*) Not you: Aurek's made a
spectacle of himself, he'll call!

He hangs up as Alexander enters, having just tripped
over. Suit, buttonhole.

What are you doing, Alex? Are you all right?

Alexander Stupid old –

Aurek Did you hurt yourself?

Alexander I mean, what sort of bag is that, what's she
got in it –?

Aurek Are you OK?

Alexander Left it right where everybody –

Aurek stifles a laugh.

Shut up. I've sprained something.

Aurek Serves you right for coming, I told you not to.

Laughter from outside.

Alexander They're laughing at me.

Aurek That's a work suit. That's not what you were going to wear.

Alexander I've got a London Assembly scrutiny this afternoon with street artists on the realities, risks and costs of graffiti, I didn't want to wear white.

Aurek You said you'd take the day off.

Alexander So did you.

Aurek I am off as soon as Marco gets here.

Alexander It's a half-hour ceremony, Aurek, and I work in the building. I couldn't get out of it.

Aurek Why didn't you tell me?

Alexander Because I knew you'd be upset.

Aurek Well, how sneaky are you? What about the drinks afterwards?

Alexander holds out a buttonhole.

Alexander Take it.

Aurek ?

Alexander A buttonhole – for your suit.

Aurek Oh. I'm not wearing one.

Alexander ?

Aurek I've got a surprise! Champagne?

Alexander Oh, Aurek. Nothing tacky. What is it?

Aurek A tattoo of your name on my shoulder.

Alexander You are joking?

Aurek Would there be something wrong with that?

Alexander Yes, it would be permanent.

Aurek Like us.

Alexander God, you're so . . . Please tell me you haven't.

Aurek I haven't.

Alexander Right. City Hall, 10.30 for 10.45.

Aurek You are coming to the drinks, aren't you?

Alexander I'll try. Stop looking so crestfallen, Aurek. Ken Livingstone's our Matron of Honour, that's how special we are. Find a suit. Just . . . nothing OTT, please. There might even be press. No statements, not today.

Aurek The GLA member for Lambeth: he likes to party.

Alexander Lambeth and Southwark. He does. I do.

His phone vibrates. He answers.

Yes? – Thames Gateway. – I don't care what they say, I've already told you to tell them: no. (*He snaps his phone shut.*)

Beat.

Aurek Could you sack whoever that was, if you felt like it?

Alexander can't resist a smile.

Could you, Alex? Send 'em packing?

Alexander You mean . . . sacrifice them like an utter bastard and say it was for the greater public good? Abso-fucking-lutely.

Aurek growls. Suddenly, he is on Alexander's face.
Alexander reciprocates, mutual intensity. Hands in
hair, cutlery on the floor.

They'll see –

Kiss.

Aurek, they'll see –

Kiss. Alexander's phone vibrates. He answers.

Ken, good morning. – Yes, yes, I've heard. – I'm just
having breakfast. – Tooley Street. – A muffin. – Bye.

Kiss.

Stop.

He detaches himself.

I'll see you shortly.

He makes to leave. He is stopped short by May's hat.

What is that?

Aurek It's a hat.

Alexander It's got a parrot in it.

Aurek So it has.

Alexander That is contemptible.

Aurek The parrot's dead.

Alexander That is not the point.

Aurek Don't panic, Alex, it belongs to that woman out
there.

Alexander She can't go round wearing things like that.

Aurek I think it's marvellous.

Alexander Taxidermy is not marvellous.

Aurek And every wedding needs a hat, Alex.

Alexander Stop calling it a wedding.

Aurek Every civil partnership registration ceremony needs a hat. Go on, put it on. I dare you.

He gulps some champagne and exits. Alexander stares after him. A moment. Aurek returns with a coffee cup, muttering to himself.

'Do you have a tomato and mozzarella panini coming for me?' I don't know, cocksucker of Bermondsey, do I?

He puts a tomato and mozzarella panini in the toaster.

Alexander Panino.

Aurek What?

Alexander Graffiti scrutiny, plural –

Aurek You have to get out of that!

Alexander – there are graffiti, there is graffito. One panino, two panini.

Aurek stares, then laughs at him.

Aurek Three panini, four . . .

Alexander Goodbye.

Aurek Sit down, let me make you a cappuccini.

He laughs. He works. Alexander watches.

Alexander You're too young.

Aurek Where are we going on our honeymoon?

Alexander Do your friends say I'm too old?

Aurek Don't leave me this way-hey-hey-hey . . .

Alexander Everyone says you're a baby.

Aurek Who cares about everyone?

Alexander It's ringing in my ears: jail-bait.

Aurek Shut up. Just shut up. This is what I want.

Beat.

It's like you're frightened of me or something. Don't worry, maybe we'll all be blown up and it won't even happen.

Alexander ?

Aurek No flights. The Chop House chef's in Manchester. They called and asked me to do the lunch shift, but *I* said no. Bye then, go, deal with your graffito.

He busies himself crossly.

Alexander We can do this.

Beat.

I just thought a buttonhole would be . . .

Beat.

I'm going to steal this hat.

Aurek Yeah, right.

Alexander It's not complicated: I'll just pick it up, put it on, march straight to work.

Aurek Whatever.

Alexander I'm going to steal this contemptible parrot hat.

He puts the hat on, and exits. Aurek is stunned. He smirks, then laughs. He feigns work as May enters hysterically, the cloth bag slung over her shoulder.

May The Deputy Mayor of London stole my hat!

Aurek What?

She shouts outside.

May Simon, Simon, come back –!

She turns back frantically to Aurek.

Did you see that man?!

Aurek shakes his head.

I know you did! I left it in here, didn't I? Call the police!

Aurek That wasn't the Deputy Mayor.

May Yes it was.

Aurek The Deputy Mayor's white.

May How do you know what the Deputy Mayor is? And Rossetti's wife didn't OD on laudanum, she drank your coffee! And where's Gilliver's breakfast? (*She holds out her hand.*) I'll have it, numbskull!

Aurek takes the panini out of the toaster. He wraps it; she shoves it in her shoulder-bag.

Aurek This isn't my shift . . .

May He was a man in a Vanessa Bell hat. Vanessa was the sister of Virginia Woolf, you'll've heard of her. Or maybe not, Polack.

Aurek Now that's just racist.

May Oh, don't talk to me about racism. Oh, at last. Marco! (*As she exits:*) Marco, the Deputy Mayor of London stole my hat!

TWO

Mid-morning. Inside City Hall: the viewing gallery.
A spacious public room with multiple entrances.
Tourists and civil servants. Towering windows to the
Thames. Some distance from the windows, a bench, on
which is Aurek, red-eyed, wearing the 'Just Registered'
T-shirt, no long jacket, no plaster. Something is tied to his
ankle. He's twirling the buttonhole fixatedly. Toni and
Patrick are at the windows, separated from Aurek by a
shaft of sunlight, contemplating the view. Toni is wearing
her short skirt and a long maroon jacket. The jacket is
very cool, but helps to conceal her prosthetic. Patrick is
wearing a jacket and tie. Her shoulder-bag and his
briefcase are nearby. She half-croons one of her folk
songs.

Toni
A bridge, Ma, up to the skies;
Look, Ma, no trainin' wheels.
At last you're wise, Isla, at last you're . . .

She drops the words and wah-wahs to a cadence. She
smiles at Patrick. He smiles back.

It's beautiful . . . and ugly. It's both. Don't you think?

She stares out. Patrick looks at his watch.

Patrick I'd better go.

Toni Yeah.

Patrick Are you off?

Toni I want to stay for a bit.

Patrick What about the Kinks?

Toni Those places are in songs: they're not going
anywhere. And I like it here, somehow.

68

Behind them Angus enters with his backpack, guitar in its cover and an Evening Standard *with the headline 'Heathrow Closed'.*

Angus So where's the Mayor when he's at home?

He piles his gear close to Aurek and looks about. Patrick points left.

Patrick Follow those buildings for London Bridge.

Toni nods. Patrick kisses her on the cheek and exits; she watches him. She gazes up into the building, moving as she does, not realising the briefcase has been left behind. She looks out at the view. Angus sits near Aurek and rolls a roll-up.

Angus Walk past every day, never been inside. Thought I'd better before they deport me.

Aurek, still twirling the buttonhole, doesn't respond.

'Just Registered.' What does that mean?

Aurek Hmn? Oh. You know . . . sort of, married.

Angus Oh, OK. When?

Aurek When they can find another window.

Angus ?

Aurek You only get thirty minutes, it's the rules. Even if you know someone.

Angus You mean . . . you can get married here?

Aurek More 'civil-partnershipped'.

Angus Sounds a bit dodgy, dude.

Aurek Very.

Angus So this is like a registry office? For anyone?

Aurek Even the gays.

Angus Ah, gotcha.

Aurek You can pick up a leaflet at information –

Angus Thanks, mate, I'm pretty right.

Aurek – there's a photo on the front of the Deputy Mayor surrounded by lesbians.

Angus Sweet.

Aurek A tiny cock amongst hens.

Angus So where's your . . . other half?

Aurek Haven't got a clue where the silly bitch is.

Angus Oooh. Nasty. You mean she's jilted you?

Aurek I couldn't think of the word. Yeah, that's it. Jilted.

Angus Shit, dude.

Aurek pulls up an arm of his T-shirt to reveal a tattoo. Angus looks closely.

'Alex.'

Aurek I've been hiding it for two weeks. I surprised . . . her . . . just next to the map of the congestion charge extension on the first floor. She loves the congestion charge extension. But this freaked her out.

Angus Fuck, dude. Now you're branded.

Aurek twirls the buttonhole. Angus strikes a match. He notices the briefcase.

Psst. Mate? Is that yours?

Aurek shakes his head. Beat.

Are you worried about it, at all?

Aurek shakes his head.

Nah, me neither.

Beat. Angus is worried. Worry turns to anxiety.

Briefcase *briefcase* BRIEFCASE.

Toni turns.

Yours?!

Toni registers it, and contains her surprise.

Toni No . . . it's all right, though, I know whose it is. Don't panic. I'll call.

She approaches it.

Angus (*to Aurek*) Some people.

He lights up, walks to the windows, and half-shouts back to Aurek.

Quite a panorama. That's my patch down there. Work there most days.

He returns.

Do you want to buy a bird whistle? Seventy-five p.

Aurek What for?

Angus I dunno, dude – blow on it and see.

He collects his gear. He offers Aurek the Standard. *Aurek takes it. Angus exits. He enters.*

Listen, man, if I could just get Johnny Depp on you for a sec: I don't have tats myself, but I had this nutter of an uncle, right, who had this illness called alexia. People with alexia can't read. They can't even see words. So you could just put an 'i' and an 'a' on the end – alex*ia* – and then you'd sort of be making the point that you wish nobody could read your bird's appellation, branded there on your deltoid for eternity.

During this, Toni kneels and tries to open the briefcase via the combination lock.

OK, that's bullshit . . . what I wanted to say is . . . you're worth more. The Vegas quickie is, like, just wrong. Get married in a church, that's what your chick's after. I speak from experience, though mine only lasted a year. She buggered off to Thailand. It cut me up, but we did it properly at the start – a special day's important, dude.

Aurek puts his hand to his face.

Oh, don't do that –

He is distracted by Toni, and steps into her sunlight.

Do you mind me asking whose briefcase you're trying to break into?

Toni ?

Angus Are they close to you? Could you conceivably have mutual *aides-mémoire*?

Toni half-nods.

Then don't think of one to do with them – think of one to do with you.

She regards him and considers this. Angus turns back to Aurek mouthing 'fucking lunatic' and gesturing 'I am out of here.'

Cheer up. I'll be just down there, OK? Wave.

He exits. Toni mutters.

Toni 4-1-2-1. 1-9-6-8. 9-9-9-4. (*Nothing. She thinks.*) 4-5-9-4. (*She revises the thought.*) 5-4-9-4.

It opens. Shock. She picks out a black diary and reads.

She finds a gift wrapped in distinctive paper and a folded patterned designer shirt. Odd. She picks out a flat digital camera. Aurek has his head in his hand.

Excuse me?

Aurek ?

Toni Would you mind?

Aurek Er . . . sure . . .

Toni hands him the camera. He stands but doesn't move.

Toni What's the name of the phallus?

Aurek The Gherkin.

Toni Make that prominent.

She randomly plucks a fake purple-white flower from the briefcase. She puts it in her hair, rests the open briefcase on her forearm and poses.

'Me in City Hall. With your detritus.'

Aurek takes the photograph.

Thank you.

On the air, pianissimo, a bird whistle. Aurek walks to the windows, revealing a daisy-chain of tin cans tied to his ankle. They drag; he cuts a mournful figure. He's now separated from Toni by space and sunlight. Toni kneels at the briefcase. Her phone rings.

Hi. – Don't panic, it's where you left it. – In the viewing gallery, I'm still here. – OK.

She hangs up. Beat. She frisks the entire briefcase and finds a boxing glove. She puts everything back in neatly, except the glove, which she puts in her shoulder-bag. She sits on the bench. Aurek half-waves to someone outside. May enters, muttering absent-mindedly. Seeing her, Aurek freezes. He shields his face with the Evening Standard.

May Mayor . . . the Mayor . . .

Patrick rushes in, out of breath, his tie slightly loose. He sees Toni immediately.

Patrick Thank God. Thank God.

May 'Tussy Marx' rhymes with 'pussy Marx' not 'fussy Marx' . . .

She exits aimlessly. Toni holds out the briefcase.

Toni Very unlike you.

Patrick What was I thinking?

Toni Nervous about your meeting, obviously . . .

Patrick nods urgently.

Patrick Now I'm running really late.

Toni Hold on.

She tightens his tie.

Did you take this off?

Patrick shakes his head.

It's odd.

Patrick ?

Toni I don't know this place at all, I don't know London. But right now, I feel like I've been dug out of the soil. I'm placed and happy. Everything I need, in this weird glassy pod. I know every joist and bolt. I shaped them. I stop it from shattering.

Aurek is on the lookout for May.

Patrick Bye.

Toni Patrick. Cancel. Come on the walking tour with me. Dirty Old River, Waterloo . . .

Patrick Where Terry finds Julie.

Toni Yeah. Actually, no: he meets her.

Patrick Faber and Faber, Toni. Promising.

Toni nods. She indicates the briefcase.

Toni Got your manuscript?

Patrick Yeah. Well, the Hong Kong edition.

Toni Jesus, your life's so *Spinal Tap*. Have we got an amp that goes to eleven? Sorry.

Patrick No, it's funny. You're funny. Thank God you stayed. I panicked. Thank you.

Toni Well, my day ends at Ray Davies' studios in Hornsey. I dunno where the fuck that is, it sounds like the asshole of England, but if you want me it's where I'll be.

She kisses him. It's charged.

Go get 'em.

Patrick rushes out. The bird whistle. Toni takes off her jacket, fully and proudly revealing her prosthetic, and lets it drop to the ground. She puts on a pair of dark sunglasses from her shoulder-bag. She lets loose a cry and strides out after Patrick. Aurek is on his own. The coast seems clear. He sees Toni's long maroon jacket. He picks it up, starts to follow her, then puts it on instead. He shoves the buttonhole in the lapel, as if to say 'Satisfied, Alexander?' May appears again, her hands on her hatless head. Aurek retreats.

May 'I remember when a few dozen of us came to Hyde Park to demand an Eight Hours Bill . . .'

Suddenly, the muffled sound of the helicopter. Peculiar shadows. She watches it through the windows. Aurek peeps.

Police, police . . .

The noise diminishes, the light adjusts itself.

Where is Ken Livingstone? The head of the Mayor . . . Bring me the head of Livingstone . . .

She exits.

Aurek Weekes . . . his gutless deputy . . . bring me the balls of Alexander fucking Weekes . . .

He reaches down, picks up a can and uses it to hit his forehead a few times. Blood. He puts his hand to the self-inflicted injury and holds back tears. He stumbles off in the opposite direction to May, Standard *under arm, hand over eye, cans dragging behind.*

THREE

Early afternoon. Outdoors at the restaurant.
A different perspective: Simon and Patrick's table is less prominent, and the scene now extends to an outdoor waiters' station. Simon and Patrick are at the table as before. Patrick is wearing the patterned designer shirt. He has his back to the station. He has just got his credit card from the wallet in his briefcase. Simon is in his Next suit. He's under the table fumbling through his Next bag for cash – during this he will accidentally spill his keys on the floor. Aurek is in the Chop House uniform and is wearing the plaster.

Aurek Well, sir, I had the shit kicked out of me. By my fiancé.

Patrick Fiancé?

Aurek Someone with authority who'd condemn that kind of thing in public. And on top of everything else now I'm stuck with her appellation injected into my skin for eternity.

This leaves Patrick nonplussed. Simon sits up and slams some notes down.

Simon I like to pay for my own raw meat when I can. (*To Aurek*) I don't need change.

Aurek picks up the money and moves to his station, where he attends to payment as Patrick and Simon's conversation continues:

Patrick Simon.

He holds out his hand. Simon shakes it.

I'm very sorry I thought you were someone else. But it's been good to catch up. You were a very good Puck.

Aurek has counted the money: Simon has left a sizeable tip.

Aurek (*to himself*) Fuck me.

Simon Thank you, Patrick. You weren't.

Patrick Good luck.

Aurek accidentally knocks a glass to the floor. It smashes. Patrick turns to look.

Simon Very clumsy, the Poles.

Aurek (*to himself*) Shit.

He gets a dustpan and brush.

Simon Oh look, and he's down on his knees already.

Beat.

Good luck with your Brando biography.

He nods to the gift.

Please. May I?

Patrick shrugs and drinks. Simon picks up the gift and unwraps it.

Look at that. *Brando: a Life*, by Patrick Mulligan.

Patrick Goodbye.

Simon And you've inscribed it. 'To Simon. My old Lysander. Patrick.'

Patrick Goodbye.

Simon How sweet.

Something else was on the table, hidden under the book. Simon picks it up. It's the fake purple-white flower. It confuses him for a moment. Then he registers recognition.

Churl, upon thy eyes I throw
All the power this charm doth owe.
When thou wakest let love forbid
Sleep his seat on thy eyelid.

Um.

Beat.

I don't remember lines from films. Someone tells me a joke, it goes. That's eighteen-year-old verse, to me. Look what you stole from the prop table . . . what you kept all this time. A little bit of Puck. His flower, yeah? Am I right? He squeezes juice into Lysander's eyes with it, hmn? The cause of all the fucking confusion?

Patrick is silent. He remains at the table as Simon picks up his Next bag and moves off, taking the book and the flower. Patrick drinks a glass and pours another. Simon walks past Aurek, who is still on all fours brushing up the glass.

(*Irish accent*) That's right, Bottom, spread yourself.

Aurek What?

Simon You heard. The Travel Inn on Tower Bridge Road for dirty afternoon shagging. £79.95.

Aurek stands and blurts this out:

Aurek I spat in your coffee.

Simon ?

Aurek I spat in your coffee this morning. I've just realised it was yours. I'm sorry. This is a big tip. I can't take this, if I spat in your coffee.

Simon is speechless.

You didn't say thanks.

Simon I did.

Aurek No . . . you just kind of ordered, then kind of left.

Simon I didn't, I wouldn't, I always say thank you. I'm queen of excuse-me-if-you'd-be-so-kind-may-I-please . . . How could you . . . take away someone's choice like that?

Aurek You've never worked as a waiter, then?

Simon It's rape.

Aurek Come on, no.

Simon I know a woman who got herpes, you hear, herpes, because some scumbag maître d' tossed off in her noodles.

79

Aurek I was nervous, it was a big day for me.

Simon Why was it bigger than mine?

Aurek I was about to get married.

Simon A jittery bride gobbed in my Americano?

Aurek Cappuccino.

Simon Well, I hope your first child is a masculine child, bitch.

Aurek He changed his mind.

Simon Good: we don't need to get wedlocked, you stupid straight-aping wanker. I never want to see you again.

He walks off. Aurek follows.

Aurek (*re the tip*) Please, this is too big.

Simon Piss off.

Aurek Wait! The old woman's hat!

Simon stops.

When you recognised me before: that woman you mentioned – from the café? You know her? It's just . . . she says she lost her hat. If you see her could you say I haven't seen it?

Simon The gobbing Polish waiter hasn't seen the hat. Right.

Aurek I'm not Polish.

Simon ?

Aurek People seem to think I'm Polish today.

Simon You said Krakow.

Aurek I lied.

Simon ?

Aurek It's easier sometimes in this job.

Simon He complimented you on Krakow.

Aurek Well, Krakow is beautiful. Tell her. It might turn up.

Simon walks off.

Wait!

Simon turns.

I could get you a doggy bag?

Simon walks off.

Wait!

Simon turns.

The raw steak wasn't deliberate.

Simon Why should I believe a single word you say?

He exits. Aurek looks towards Patrick. He is drinking back another glass. During the above he has picked up a set of keys from the floor. He jangles them. Aurek approaches.

Aurek Can I get you anything else, sir?

Patrick Your name. That's what I'd like.

Aurek Was the service satisfactory, sir?

Patrick Yes. I just want to call you whatever you're called.

Aurek You don't need to do that.

Patrick Pity.

He puts the keys on the table.

The man I had lunch with, I think. He must have dropped them.

Aurek looks towards Simon's exit and attempts to pick up the keys. Patrick puts his hand on top of Aurek's to stop him.

Too late.

He fills his glass.

(*To himself*) Jesus.

He drinks.

And I don't know where he lives.

Aurek Do you have his number?

Patrick How long can I stay?

Aurek Do you have his number?

Patrick Another bottle of Château Montus.

Aurek Sir, the gentleman's keys –

Patrick Let me see.

He gets his phone out and scrolls.

Simon Gilliver . . . Simon Gilliver . . .

Aurek Simon Gilliver?

Patrick I got his number from Josh Allen. Yes. There he is.

He puts the phone on the table and drinks.

Aurek You could leave the keys here, sir; he might come back for them.

Patrick Do you know a half-decent hotel nearby? Not too pricey.

Aurek The Travel Inn on Tower Bridge Road, £79.95.

Patrick Oh. How efficient. It didn't occur to me you were so obviously rent. Good.

Aurek I think you might have had a bit too much, sir.

Patrick Would you like to come with me?

Aurek No.

He clears a glass.

Patrick No. No. (*Whispering to himself.*) Jesus wept. Fucking Christ. God help me.

Beat.

I fucked a boy.

Beat.

I'd forgotten it. On my life, I'd forgotten it.

Aurek looks around, uncomfortable.

I don't know what I've done. Why did I hold on to a name like that and muddle it? I got bladdered every night with Lysander and fucked around with him, that's all I remembered. But he says I did something. Like a paedophile. I was twenty . . . that's all. (*He taps his head.*) Something's wrong. Jesus, fuck. A mistake, an error.

Aurek Er, Château Montus, sir?

Patrick I don't remember what I remember.

Aurek Sir?

Patrick Drugs. For the Travel Inn. What've you got?

Aurek I –

Patrick Me, just a filthy bottle of blueies.

Aurek Your meal's been paid for, sir.

Patrick Because even depravity runs out of life.

Aurek Perhaps you should go.

Patrick Bring me another bottle of Château Montus. Another one, I tell you. (*He drinks.*) I need a piss.

Aurek Through there, to the –

Patrick knows the way and walks off. His briefcase, keys and mobile phone are still on the table. Aurek looks around, then pockets the keys quickly. He picks up Patrick's mobile, scrolls, and with a pen from his pocket copies a number on the bill receipt, then pockets this. He puts the phone back and begins to clear Simon's cutlery. Alexander enters. He's holding an Armani bag. He's not wearing the buttonhole. Aurek stares.

Alexander Good God, what happened to your forehead? Are you all right?

Beat.

Aurek I'm telling people you did it. I thought it'd make me feel better. It doesn't. What are you doing here?

Alexander I've come to say sorry.

Aurek You have to go.

Aurek moves to the waiters' station. Alexander follows.

Alexander Who did you tell I hit you . . . ?

Aurek Alex: leave.

Alexander holds out the Armani bag.

Alexander Take it.

Aurek Don't you get it? I'd never wear that.

Alexander You haven't even seen it.

Aurek Nor have you. Why is it you think you can barge in on my work? I wouldn't do it to you.

Alexander That's not true, is it? Three or four of my colleagues saw you making a complete fool of yourself in front of the Chamber this morning with those idiotic cans around your ankle. I told you to leave.

Beat.

Look at this place, it's empty.

Aurek It was me: I walk into a room, it clears.

Alexander Yes.

Beat.

Don't change.

Beat.

I got caught up.

Aurek I saw this helicopter, it came really low, and I thought, he's on it, he's dust, I'll never see him.

Alexander It's a bad day. It wasn't possible.

Aurek You see, I don't think that's the truth.

Patrick makes his way back to the table and sits.

Alexander God, I could fuck you right here and now.

Aurek No, Alexander, that's a pile of crap.

Alexander It scares the life out of me, because I could.

Patrick (*calling*) Château Montus!

He accidentally knocks some cutlery off the table.

Aurek We've had it in the diary for *six months*.

He gets the wine.

Alexander That bloke's pissed as a newt.

Aurek That bloke's a paedophile.

Alexander What?

Aurek That's what he says.

Alexander You're kidding?

Aurek No, I just made it up.

Alexander Aurek. Did he say that?

Aurek Yeah.

Alexander And? What are you going to do?

Aurek I've had enough –

Alexander You have to ring the –

Aurek Just go, Deputy Do-Good, please.

Alexander My God, Aurek?

Aurek According to the *Evening Standard* the plane thing's down to computers. Is it?

Alexander I don't know any more than they do.

Aurek Would you travel on the tube today?

Alexander I wouldn't travel on the tube any day.

Aurek I should ring the *Daily Mail* with that.

Alexander Never joke about collaborating with the *Mail*.

Beat.

It is what it is, nothing. Forget it. People are sheep.

Aurek takes the bottle to Patrick's table. He opens it as Alexander takes a call on his mobile.

Weekes? – Five minutes.

Patrick (*to Aurek*) Join me?

Aurek shakes his head. He pours a glass. Patrick drinks it down. Aurek pours another, then goes back to the waiters' station.

Aurek I'm going to lose this job, and it'll be your fault. Not that jobs for waiters are hard to get.

Alexander It's all right, I'm going.

Aurek Before you do – what happened to the parrot hat?

Alexander I dumped it.

Aurek You what? Where?

Alexander In a bin.

Aurek Why?

Alexander Because I'm morally opposed to blood sports and didn't want a stuffed animal in my office.

Aurek You're such an idiot, Alex, what if that old woman knows who you are?

Alexander Unfortunately, she does. She's been making a nuisance of herself in City Hall all day. They caught her and threw her out, thank God. I managed to laugh it off to security; luckily, she seems completely certifiable.

Beat.

Take the shirt.

Aurek We didn't need a piece of paper. We'd only need another one for our gay divorce, wouldn't we? I'm right, aren't I?

Alexander Look, do you want me to tell you it's because you turned up looking like a, like a, weirdo? That ridiculous T-shirt . . . and customising yourself like a tin of baked beans?

Aurek This is me. It's me.

Alexander And I didn't want my colleagues to see it. I didn't want anyone to see it.

Beat.

I'll try to come home early, I'll get something from Marks for dinner.

Aurek If I eat one more thing from Marks and Spencer's I'm going to heave, I just want to get a carrot and wash it and peel it and chop it *myself.*

Alexander Put the diva back in the bag, Aurek. Fine: cook.

Aurek Fuck you.

He throws Simon's half-empty glass over Alexander's suit. Alexander remains sad and calm.

Alexander I've got a scrutiny hearing.

Aurek I suppose this means Red Ken isn't going to be joining us tonight for a spit-roast?

Alexander puts his hand on Aurek's arm gently.

I wanted to do this today. You're not too old for me, Alex, you're not.

He kisses him. Alexander is impassive.

Alexander You'll lose your job.

Aurek I don't care.

Alexander I'm sorry. I don't know what I was thinking. I have to go.

Aurek You've done this, Alex. Not me.

Alexander You were right. You scare the life out of me. I haven't got what it takes inside to be so . . .

Aurek Public.

Beat.

Hypocrite. Look around. See what's happening. There's nothing wrong with it.

Alexander *Bocsánat.*

Aurek Don't you speak in my language.

Alexander I'm sorry.

He exits. Aurek stands still, tears welling. Alexander returns.

Aurek Oh, bloody hell, Alex, what are you trying to do to me –?

Alexander Look, that man . . . is that what he told you? Did he say that, Aurek? Answer.

Aurek Yes.

Alexander Keep him here. Don't let him go, all right? And remember everything he said.

He puts the Armani bag down and exits. Aurek pulls himself together. He returns to Patrick's table to top up his glass. Patrick stops him. He is now mournfully drunk.

Patrick That's it. Enough.

He puts money down for the last bottle. Aurek takes it to the waiters' station. Patrick unlocks the briefcase to put his wallet and phone inside. Something catches his eye. He searches; something is missing. He picks up the flat digital camera. He presses a button. Shock. He looks about wildly.

Where are you? Where is she?

Aurek returns.

Toni?

Aurek Sir?

Patrick Where?

He slams the briefcase shut and puts his elbows on it. He laughs, eerily.

So you're getting married?

Aurek One day.

Patrick And you let your wife clobber you?

Aurek No.

Patrick Oh, don't be ashamed. I have a wife. I love her, I do . . . I love her. She keeps me . . . on a path. She would clobber me, if she could. I need her. I need her to keep me . . . keep me . . .

He can't convey it, and gestures feebly: 'steady', 'normal', 'on the straight and narrow'.

She needs me, too. I'm someone to hate. Yes, I mean that. I know when it started: 1994, April. I didn't know something. There was a popular footnote I'd let slide, she's never forgiven me. It made her start hating me. The not-knowing of something began to put a line between us, marked me as a particular kind of opponent. She'd say she hates me because I fuck around, but that's not it. It's because of April 1994. I'd booked this restaurant in Raleigh. She was late, and she looked awful, so anguished, as if somebody had died. Turned out, somebody had. 'Who?' I said. 'Who, my darling?' And she said, 'Kurt,' and I thought, well I don't know any Kurts, she's never mentioned a Kurt to me before, who the fuck is Kurt?

Apparently, I have a problem with names. So I simply asked, 'Kurt who?' Reasonable question. I got my answer: 'Cobain, you idiot, who do you think? Dead.' And she sat. Gaping at her fork. As if our little baby girl was dead inside her tummy.

Aurek Well, it was a sad day.

Patrick Jesus Christ, you must have been three.

Aurek Thirteen. I was at school in Canada. During French all the girls were wailing tears that weren't wet.

Patrick Well. I was none the wiser. 'Who's Kurtis Cobain?' I said, and I said it sweetly – I mean he might have been Toni's uncle or her old guitar teacher – it had to be someone she knew, right, someone she knew and loved? I was so worried, because I loved her, and she pretends to be hard, to have skin like animal hide, but she isn't hard, so I gently muttered, 'Who's Kurtis Cobain?' 'Kurt, Kurt, Kurt you fucking immigrant, Kurt Cobain,' and she hit the fork with her fist and it went flying into someone's chowder and we had to leave.

Aurek It was a sad day, and that seems rude, but maybe she was just venting steam over the dawning realisation she'd married a homosexual.

Beat.

Patrick Apparently everyone knew who he was except me. A whole generation was shell-shocked, apparently. Somehow I'd missed out. And I'm a very cool person. I own Marlon Brando's boxing glove. Oh, yes. It's here. Somewhere. But Kurt just slipped me by. And I called him Kurtis. And she started loving to hate me.

Beat.

A year later when Jerry Garcia died I was fucking prepared.

Beat.

I read about an educated middle-class Englishwoman, with children, who'd never heard of Winnie-the-Pooh.

He runs his finger along the briefcase.

Fifth of April, '94.

Aurek Or perhaps, the realisation she'd married a paedophile?

Beat.

Patrick It's only him, only him, and he's gay. I'm not that, no. I've done some horrible things, from leaving my girl alone to shoving Marlon Brando's boxing glove up some piece of trade's arse –

Aurek (*disgusted*) Oh, for God's sake –

Patrick I can say I did those things. Because I did. But I don't know, I don't know. I remember Simon Gilliver. Cocksure little . . . thing. Cocksure. Cocksure. And eyes. Adoring eyes.

Beat.

Oh, I see. God, his blue eyes . . . by the car . . . in the mirror.

He is weeping.

Does this shirt suit me?

Aurek I don't –

Patrick I was a kid.

Silent tears. Aurek doesn't really know what to do. Patrick grabs Aurek's arm.

Don't say anything. Please. I'll sort it out. I'll slit my wrists, that's what I'll do. I've fucked so many people I can't even remember who's who, I'll open my wrists.

Aurek shakes him off. Beat.

Aurek Coffee?

Patrick No.

Aurek Cognac?

Patrick Where's she hiding? Where is she?

He rips open his cuffs and pops the top button of his shirt as if wanting to tear it off. He takes off his watch and slings it on the table. He gets up and staggers off, very slowly.

Which way to the boats?

Aurek Come back . . .

Patrick Down the river . . .

He leaves everything: watch, briefcase, wallet, phone.

Aurek Sir . . . your . . . sir –

He tries to stop him but Patrick pushes him away. He disappears along the water. Aurek isn't sure what to do. On the table, Patrick's mobile rings. Aurek looks towards Patrick, already a speck, then registers who is calling on ID.

Hello? – Yes, hello. – It's not Patrick. – It's Aurek, the waiter. Wait, don't hang up. – Aurek. – Listen to me, I've got your – Huh?

He pulls the phone back from his ear suddenly. The sound of the bird whistle comes through. It stops. He puts his phone back to his ear. He hangs up. He stares out front.

FOUR

Dusk. Potters Fields.

Tall shadows. The bench, bin and tree are now in the distance; other trees, etc., obscure them. Aurek has the Armani bag and a large Le Pont de la Tour foodstore bag. He's wearing the jacket, no buttonhole, but it's been cut in half: it's now a short jacket. He's buttoned it at the front. Like everything on Aurek, it's effortlessly cool. He has the plaster above his eye. May's sitting on a bench, asleep. She's wearing her summer hat trimmed with parrot and peach. Her cloth bag is at her feet. Simon is next to her. He has the Next bag. He's in his Cockfighter of Bermondsey T-shirt. He has a black eye. He's reading a book; the fake flower is his bookmark. Toni and Angus are somewhere in the trees. Chilled-out music from their guitar. Simon looks up as Aurek approaches.

Simon Hi.

Aurek Hi.

Simon How's things?

Aurek You know, the same.

Simon Still rabidly homosexual, then?

Aurek Oh, yeah.

Simon Electric shock treatment didn't work?

Aurek Dead loss, my friend, total washout.

Simon Can't win 'em all.

Aurek I think there are places I can go to find happiness. Hairdressers. Anglican churches. Asda.

Simon I've heard some rumours. One can't be sure. Trust no one.

Aurek There's a secret handshake.

Simon (*shaking his head*) Urban myth. It's a trap.

Aurek Your aversion therapy successful?

Simon (*nodding*) They zapped my lobes so hard I'm shaking like a hypothermic puppy in the rain.

Aurek Oh, bless.

Simon But now I love to eat pussy.

Aurek It's really good to hear a success story.

Simon I'm back on people's Christmas card lists. Thank you, Ministry of Love.

Beat.

Aurek What are you reading?

Simon A biography of Marlon Brando.

Aurek retches involuntarily.

Are you all right?

Aurek nods, still retching.

You don't like Brando?

Aurek coughs up spit.

Do you want some water?

Aurek shakes his head. He holds out Simon's keys. Simon takes them.

Can I get –?

Aurek shakes his head, trying to speak:

Aurek It's . . . I'm . . . (*He recovers, just.*) allergic . . .

Beat.

Simon Thanks for making the effort to get these back to me. I didn't want to have to change my locks . . . can't stand things like that. Are you sure you're all right?

Aurek nods. He looks to May.

Aurek Her hat!

Simon It was in a bin. She'd been trying to see Ken Livingstone about it all day.

Aurek She must have had her reasons.

Simon Yeah, they just didn't seem reasonable, on the face of it. I don't know: something about the Deputy Mayor? And your coffee shop? Hmn?

Aurek shrugs like a waiter.

She was prowling the corridors asking for his head. They chucked her out. She rang me. I don't know why she does that. I wish she wouldn't, really. I don't know when . . . I can't remember how I got stuck with her.

Aurek The main thing is she got her hat back.

Simon Why are you so concerned?

Aurek It's a fabulous hat.

Simon Oh, it is: with a fabulous ex-parrot.

Aurek Yeah.

Beat. He holds out the Armani bag.

It's a shirt. It's not to say sorry . . . you happen to be here and I won't wear it. It's a good one. I'm also hoping the man who got some junior civil servant to buy it for me can see me giving it to a stranger. That's his office. Two floors down, five windows to the right.

Simon I see. Alexander Weekes?

Aurek nods.

Your boyfriend?

Aurek Not any more.

Simon So she's not completely off her chump?

Aurek No.

Simon Do you know how much grief he caused her?

Aurek It's my fault. I thought it was funny. I realised it wasn't. I'm relieved you found it. Take the shirt.

Simon I wouldn't wear it either.

Aurek 'Cause you only shop at Next?

Simon (*tugging at his Cockfighter T-shirt*) Feast your eyes on this, sunshine: this is a very cool T-shirt.

Aurek smiles.

Aurek I know.

Simon Nice jacket.

Aurek Thanks, I've just distressed it.

Beat.

Simon Well . . . bye.

Aurek Simon, would you like a drink?

Simon No. We don't like you. You make bitter coffee.

Aurek I've got no control over the coffee.

Simon Only whether you gob in it or not. Bye. Seriously: see you.

Aurek Look . . . er . . . as a waiter, I find that a lot of times when people leave things at restaurants, they actually mean to. We get all sorts of dossiers and numbers on napkins at the Chop House . . . stuff people lose so they can say it's lost. Subconscious, conscious, I dunno, but deliberate. Really, nearly always it looks important and nearly always they 'forget' to come back for it.

He takes Patrick's belongings (phone, briefcase, watch) from the Pont de la Tour bag.

Simon You got so lucky with my lunch-date you scored his belongings?

Aurek Your 'date'?

Simon What you mean to say is you stole these from the Travel Inn, where you were fucking? You answered his phone, that was his wife. What did you do, leave him strung up against the bathroom door with an orange jammed in his mouth?

Aurek Simon. I'm not lying. I'm giving these to you, but I think they should go to the police.

Simon takes them, uneasily.

Simon Right. Well. Thanks: I'll get them back to my friend, cheers, bye.

Aurek Your friend the paedophile?

Beat.

That's what he called himself.

Beat.

Look, I don't know, it's none of my business . . . But after he left, I went for a piss . . . and I couldn't piss. It was weird, I was trying –

Simon You can't if you try.

Aurek No, it was because I'd got the terrors, and it had nothing to do with my day and everything to do with

98

yours. He said he couldn't remember what he'd done. To you, right? I stood at the urinal sweating . . . shaking. I'd let him go. He just . . . walked off.

Beat.

Anyway, the cops might be on to him: I told Alexander Weekes.

Simon ?

Aurek And Alex being Alex definitely would have done the 'right' thing. I should have left it all at the Chop House. Maybe you should take it to the police?

Simon You have to keep your mouth shut.

Aurek But you don't have anything to hide.

Simon I don't want to see him again.

Aurek So why today?

Simon Because . . . because . . . who are you? You have to pretend you've never seen this, OK? That's what I want.

Aurek He walked off down the river.

Simon You wanted me to have this stuff for a reason, so listen: you've never seen it.

Aurek But was it like how he said?

Simon I want it how it was: no one knows.

Aurek OK.

Simon These things are nothing.

Aurek All right.

Simon They don't exist.

Beat. Aurek sits. Three on a bench.

Wait. That means it was the Deputy Mayor who hit you?

Aurek (*shaking his head*) I lied to the Chop House that I couldn't come in because I'd tripped in the bathroom and needed stitches, and after Alex left me at the altar, I decided to go to work. So I needed stitches.

Simon You hit yourself?

Aurek I was a bit depressed.

Simon Why didn't you just fake it? A plaster doesn't have to have a wound underneath, does it?

Aurek It was a very crap day, I didn't think of that.

Beat.

How long does she have?

Simon What sort of question's that?

Aurek She said something about being ill –?

Simon You've got that wrong.

Aurek indicates Simon's black eye.

Aurek What happened to you, anyway?

Simon I was struck in the face with Marlon Brando's boxing glove, the one he used in *The Godfather*.

Aurek retches.

Streetcar Named Desire?

Aurek retches.

On the Water – what's the matter with you?

Aurek (*raspy*) Nothing.

Simon OK then . . .

He collects Patrick's belongings.

I've got to go . . . I have to get rid of this . . .

He takes the boxing glove out of the Next bag. Aurek screams.

Aurek Put it down!

He screams.

Simon What are you on?

May wakes up.

Aurek Don't touch it!

May What's the –?

Aurek Put it down, throw it away!

May What?

Simon Stop! What is the matter with you? You crazy fucking . . . waiter? Haven't you done enough? Thank you for my keys. Now go, go, go.

May What is it?

Aurek Is it?! Is it Marlon Brando's?!

Simon Yes. Apparently.

Aurek Destroy it, destroy it.

May Marlon Brando's?

Simon (*snapping*) *On the Waterfront*, '55.

May Oh my goodness. How utterly fascinating. May I have a look?

Aurek At least wash it, wash it.

May No, you mustn't clean such things: Glenda Jackson washed her Oscar and the gold plating came off. Why have you got it?

Simon I stole it to prevent a murder.

May Of the man you had chops with?

Simon No more conspiracies, Cassandra, please.

May May I have a look?

Simon I'm burning it.

Aurek Burn the glove, burn the glove.

May I'd love to just touch –

Simon Everyone shut their fucking traps.

Beat.

It's all going back to his wife.

He gets up and walks into the distance to Toni and Angus.

May Look who it is.

Aurek Aurek.

May Yes.

Beat.

Let me tell you something, Aurek. It's very important. This is the God's honest truth. On my mother's life, may she rest in peace. I met Brando. I had a day's filming in a paranormal country house with him and Michael Winner.

The guitar music stops. She gets the tomato and mozzarella panini out of her bag and eats it.

Aurek How long have you known Simon?

May Since he bought next door.

Aurek Is he in a relationship?

May He callously killed the predators on his daisies. He went to Poland for his holidays and came back traumatised by Auschwitz. He let that beast off the hook today, from what I can glean. A mess.

Aurek Is he in a relationship?

May There was a boyfriend but people don't want to grow old together now.

Aurek I do.

May Can you spend your Sunday evenings with someone else? That's the question. When you're yoked to someone else, Sunday nights can be very taxing things. Every Sunday, for the rest of your life?

Aurek Well, yeah. On a Sunday I'd . . . light candles and chop carrots and raise kids and watch *Antiques Roadshow* and drink wine. Yeah.

May You poor boy. The noughties aren't very naughty, are they?

> *Beat.*

Aurek Everyone stops what they're doing when straight people get married. Everyone stopped for my sister.

> *Beat.*

May Were your ancestors collaborators?

Aurek What?

May Do you have a right to work in this country?

Aurek Hungary's part of the EU.

May Hungary?

Aurek Yeah. Where my father came from, before he got to Canada, where he met my mother. And none of this is any of your business.

May I'm sorry.

Aurek Are you his only friend?

May Lord, no.

Beat.

Aurek?

Aurek Yeah?

May Find out his middle name for me.

Simon returns from the trees, with Toni. She has the briefcase and the other belongings.

Simon (*to Aurek*) This is Toni Mulligan, the Irishman's wife.

Toni So you're the waiter? And apparently as pure and virginal as Gulliver?

Simon Gilliver.

Aurek Hello. Aurek –

He recognises her, and is a bit self-conscious in the stolen and hacked jacket. She throws a look at it.

Toni Where did he go?

Aurek I don't know.

Toni Where is he now, please?

Aurek I let him go. He's gone.

Toni I rang the hotel, he's not there.

Aurek He left all that behind.

Toni Twice. Very odd behaviour, for Patrick. He usually has very tight control over his bits and pieces. You played with his head, Gilliver. Something is wrong.

Aurek I'm telling the truth. He's . . . he's gone.

Simon Toni. I want to go now. I'm going home. So . . .
just . . . let him slip off, I don't care . . . Just fucking
throw it all in the fucking Thames, why don't you?

Beat.

Toni That hat is completely offensive and totally
beautiful.

May It's for a biographical picture of Vanessa Bell – she
was Virginia Woolf's sister.

Toni I know who Vanessa Bell was and not for one
second would she have condoned the slaughtering and
stuffing of parrots for millinery. You're in *The
Nightcomers*?

May I am.

Toni hands her the boxing glove.

Toni I have to tell you that I saw my husband sniffing
this, once.

Aurek swallows his vomit.

Now. I'm going to chuck the rest of this crap in Dirty
Old River, as the man suggested.

*She kneels, opens the briefcase and puts the watch and
phone inside.*

Unless any of you would like the tie I gave him for his
birthday? Or a jacket? Or some Viagra? Or the biggest
black book of fags you ever did see? Nipple-clamps? No?
I'm shocked: you're all so vanilla.

*Simon drops the Brando biography inside, followed by
the fake flower. Toni clasps it shut. She exits towards
the river. They watch. Three heads rise and fall. Three
heads look downstream.*

May It would have been such a pity if she'd been subtle; I am pleased she found the Scarlett O'Hara in that.

Toni returns, without the briefcase. Inevitably, farcically, she and Simon get in each other's way: left, right, left.

Simon Sorry.

Toni Sorry.

Simon Sorry.

Toni Asshole.

Simon Bitch.

Toni Bite me.

Simon I'm not trying to hurt you.

Toni I know that.

Simon I remember . . . I remember loving him.

Toni If that's how you've decided to make sense of your showing up for a lunch.

Simon That's not it. I had this feeling of being completely . . . hamstrung . . . by all the feeling.

Toni It's a trick of time.

Simon But I felt it again.

Toni Tell me, didn't it play the same trick on him, about someone else?

Simon You don't get it – it felt good.

Toni Wait, now you're telling me it smelled of roses? What's up with that? You suddenly remember him winking at you somewhere, do you? Choosing some line from a book just for you? Some dead-poet moment makes it all rosy, huh? Crap. He isn't more special than other people you've loved. After everything you've done

today, all of a sudden you start telling me about good
things? That's shit, and you know it; don't give me
schmaltz, Gilliver, I do the schmaltz, buster, I write the
songs, because he's been with me every day for a decade.
Locked together like dogs. There's good and there's bad,
and I fucking love bad – but if it's wrong, it's wrong.
What are you, suddenly scared you'll seem like a prig if
you say so? So what, you're a goddamn prig. The man's
rotting, I can feel it –

Simon No, I don't want that to happen to him –

Toni Shut up, it was wrong, Gilliver, OK? Shut up, wrong,
you got it?!

> *She clutches the back of his neck with her good hand
> and they lock foreheads. Eyes down, dead still.
> Solidarity, white-hot. They hold this for some time.
> Toni breaks away eventually.*

I like your tattoo. This is a lovely dusk. And that guy
plays guitar the way I do.

> *She walks back to Angus. May puts the boxing glove
> and – why not? – the Armani bag in her shoulder-bag.*

May Time to go.

Aurek (*to Simon*) You don't have to, do you?

> *Simon nods.*

Why?

Simon Um. The cleaner's coming tomorrow.

Aurek So?

Simon I've got to clean up.

Aurek What for?

Simon The cleaner.

Aurek I don't know what's worse, that you've got a cleaner, or that you clean for the cleaner.

Simon I don't clean for the cleaner.

Aurek Then what do you do?

Simon You know, straighten the magazines.

Aurek Hide the porn.

Simon I don't have porn.

Aurek laughs. So does May.

I've got to go.

Aurek restrains him with a touch. A moment.

I'm sorry I called you a cunt.

Aurek You called me a cunt twice; after a while it just doesn't hurt any more, you know?

Simon Your service was bad.

Aurek It wasn't.

Simon I'd a right to complain about raw meat, and you did kind of sneer.

Aurek I don't sneer.

Simon I really wanted to, I don't know, kill you . . . and I'm sorry because it wasn't about . . .

Aurek I know.

Simon God, I'm starving.

Aurek Let me make it up to you.

Simon How old are you?

Aurek Twenty-four.

Simon No.

The guitar music resumes. Toni sings. A simple, almost-sweet, almost-melodic almost-folk tune. Simon, May and Aurek listen.

Toni

It's all been a delusion,
You've been talkin' to thin air.
Been sleepin' with a notion –
Babe, I was never there.
So when you cried 'I love you'
That was no big deal –
You were talkin' to an abstract,
It can't walk or talk or kneel.
Ain't nothing but a figment,
It can't cough or crap or squeal.
So why, babe, do you think
That it is even real?

Angus harmonises.

Angus *and* **Toni**

Yeah why, babe, do you think
That it is even real?

Toni

'Cause I am sweet F.A.,
Can't breathe or laugh or ache.
Babe, I'm a flake of nothing,
Except your big mistake:
Forget the words you spoke,
On you, babe, is the joke,
'Cause 'nothing' can't be broke,
No, 'nothing' can't be broke.

Beat. Angus appears from the trees.

Angus She sure can kill a party, can't she? I'm really looking forward to hearing one of her pessimistic songs, aren't you?

He disappears back to Toni. Guitar music resumes. Beat.

Aurek I can feel something in my bones. The trip home's going to be hell.

Simon Yeah, that's all we ever really worry about. Something terrible happens somewhere, it just pisses us off a bit. 'Fuck, don't let that hijack my day.' All we really worry about is how we're going to get home.

May As you never set foot out of SE1, even that wouldn't worry you.

Aurek Simon?

Simon Mmn?

Aurek You've got my number – from when I called you. Save it to your contacts.

Simon Right.

Aurek Do it now.

Simon OK.

Aurek Go on then.

Simon gets his phone out and saves the number.

A-U-R-E-K. When I text, text back.

Simon Bye, Aurek.

He stands. So does May.

Aurek Ring me.

Simon I will.

Aurek No, really ring me.

Simon Yeah, whatever.

Aurek I can't believe you're going home to clean for your cleaner.

They smile at each other. Simon walks off.

May He'll be at the coffee shop first thing Monday morning.

Aurek Really?

May It's a very patterned life.

Aurek I'll swap shifts with Marco, I'll be there.

May Night, lad.

She waves.

Find out his middle name.

She pads off after Simon. Toni and Angus have been enveloped by the trees. Aurek walks off in the opposite direction to May and Simon.

The End.